THE UNKNOWN LIFE

OF

JESUS CHRIST

THE UNKNOWN LIFE

OF

JESUS CHRIST

NICOLAS NOTOVITCH

TRANSLATED BY

J. H. CONNELLY AND L. LANDSBERC

GYAN

Published by

Gyan Publishing House
5, Ansari Road
Daryaganj, New Delhi-110002
Phone: 011-47034999, 9811692060
E-mail: books@gyanbooks.com

Distribution Network
gyanbooks.com
India, USA, Canada, UK, Australia

ISBN: 978-93-6208-045-5 (HB)
First Published, 1890

2nd Impression 2024

Printed at: Gyan Press, Delhi.

THE UNKNOWN LIFE OF JESUS CHRIST
Author: NICOLAS NOTOVITCH, Translators: J. H. CONNELLY AND L. LANDSBERC

The Unknown Life

of

JESUS CHRIST

THE UNKNOWN LIFE

OF

JESUS CHRIST

By the Discoverer of the Manuscript

NICOLAS NOTOVITCH

Translated by

J. H. CONNELLY and L. LANDSBERG

R. F. FENNO & COMPANY

16 East 17 Street

NEW YORK

CONTENTS.

PREFACE.

After the Turkish War (1877–1878) I made a series of travels in the Orient. From the little remarkable Balkan peninsula, I went across the Caucasus to Central Asia and Persia, and finally, in 1887, visited India, an admirable country which had attracted me from my earliest childhood. My purpose in this journey was to study and know, at home, the peoples who inhabit India and their customs, the grand and mysterious archæology, and the colossal and majestic nature of their country. Wandering about without fixed plans, from one place to another, I came to mountainous Afghanistan, whence I regained India by way of the picturesque passes of Bolan and Guernaï. Then, going up the Indus to Raval Pindi, I ran over the Pendjab—the land of the five rivers; visited the Golden Temple of Amritsa—the tomb of the King of Pendjab, Randjid Singh, near Lahore; and turned toward Kachmyr, "The Valley of Eternal Bliss." Thence I directed my peregrinations as my curiosity impelled me, until I arrived in Ladak, whence I intended returning to Russia by way of Karakoroum and Chinese Turkestan.

One day, while visiting a Bhuddist convent on my route, I learned from a chief lama, that there existed in the archives of Lhassa, very ancient memoirs relating to the life of Jesus Christ and the occidental nations, and that certain great monasteries possessed old copies and translations of those chronicles.

As it was little probable that I should make another journey into this country, I resolved to put off my return to Europe until a later date, and, cost what it might, either find those copies in the great convents or go to Lhassa —a journey which is far from being so dangerous and difficult as is generally supposed, involving only such perils as I was already accustomed to, and which would not make me hesitate at attempting it.

During my sojourn at Leh, capital of Ladak, I visited the great convent Himis, situated near the city, the chief lama of which informed me that their monastic library contained copies of the manuscripts in question. In order that I might not awaken the suspicions of the authorities concerning the object of my visit to the cloister, and to evade obstacles which might be opposed to me as a Russian, prosecuting further my journey in Thibet, I gave out upon my return to Leh that I would depart for India, and so left the capital of Ladak. An unfortunate fall, causing the breaking of a leg, furnished me with an absolutely unexpected pretext for returning to the monastery, where I received surgical attention. I took advantage of my short sojourn among the lamas to obtain the consent of their chief that they should bring to me, from their library, the manuscripts relating to Jesus Christ, and, assisted by my interpreter, who translated for me the Thibetan language, transferred carefully to my note-book what the lama read to me.

Not doubting at all the authenticity of this

chronicle, edited with great exactitude by the Brahminic, and more especially the Buddhistic historians of India and Nepaul, I desired, upon my return to Europe, to publish a translation of it.

To this end, I addressed myself to several universally known ecclesiastics, asking them to revise my notes and tell me what they thought of them.

Mgr. Platon, the celebrated metropolitan of Kiew, thought that my discovery was of great importance. Nevertheless, he sought to dissuade me from publishing the memoirs, believing that their publication could only hurt me. "Why?" This the venerable prelate refused to tell me more explicitly. Nevertheless, since our conversation took place in Russia, where the censor would have put his veto upon such a work, I made up my mind to wait.

A year later, I found myself in Rome. I showed my manuscript to a cardinal very near to the Holy Father, who answered me literally in these words:—"What good will it do to print this? Nobody will attach to it any great importance and you will create a number of enemies. But, you are still very young! If it is a question of money which concerns you, I can ask for you a reward for your notes, a sum which will repay your expenditures and recompense you for your loss of time." Of course, I refused.

In Paris I spoke of my project to Cardinal Rotelli, whose acquaintance I had made in Constantinople. He, too, was opposed to having my work printed, under the pretext that it would be premature. "The church," he added, "suffers already too much from the new current of atheistic ideas, and you will but give a new food to the calumniators and detractors of the evangelical doctrine. I tell you this in the interest of all the Christian churches."

Then I went to see M. Jules Simon. He found my matter very interesting and advised me to ask the opinion of M. Renan, as to the best way of publishing these memoirs. The next day I was seated in the cabinet of the great philosopher. At the close of our conversation, M. Renan proposed that I should confide to him the memoirs in question, so that he might make to the Academy a report upon the discovery.

This proposition, as may be easily understood, was very alluring and flattering to my *amour propre.* I, however, took away with me the manuscript, under the pretext of further revising it. I foresaw that if I accepted the proposed combination, I would only have the honor of having found the chronicles, while the illustrious author of the "Life of Jesus" would have the glory of the publication and the commenting upon it. I thought myself sufficiently prepared to publish the translation of the chronicles, accompanying them with my notes, and, therefore, did not accept the very gracious offer he made to me. But, that I might not wound the susceptibility of the great master, for whom I felt a profound respect, I made up my mind to delay publication until after his death, a fatality which could not be far off, if I might judge from the apparent general weakness of M. Renan. A short time after M. Renan's death, I wrote to M. Jules Simon again for his advice. He answered me, that it was my affair to judge of the opportunity for making the memoirs public.

I therefore put my notes in order and now publish them, reserving the right to substantiate the authenticity of these chronicles. In my commentaries I proffer the arguments which must convince us of the sincerity and good faith of the Buddhist compilers. I wish to add that before criticising my communication, the societies of *savans* can, without much expense, equip a scientific expedition having for its mission the study of those manuscripts in the place where I discovered them, and so may easily verify their historic value.

NICOLAS NOTOVITCH.

THE UNKNOWN LIFE OF JESUS CHRIST.

A JOURNEY IN THIBET.

During my sojourn in India, I often had occasion to converse with the Buddhists, and the accounts they gave me of Thibet excited my curiosity to such an extent that I resolved to make a journey into that still almost unknown country. For this purpose I set out upon a route crossing Kachmyr (Cashmere), which I had long intended to visit.

On the 14th of October, 1887, I entered a railway car crowded with soldiers, and went from Lahore to Raval-Pindi, where I arrived the next day, near noon. After resting a little and inspecting the city, to which the permanent garrison gives the aspect of a military camp, I provided myself with the necessaries for a journey, where horses take the place of the railway cars. Assisted by my servant, a colored man of Pondichery, I packed all my baggage, hired a tonga (a two-wheeled vehicle which is drawn by two horses), stowed myself upon its back seat, and set out upon the picturesque road leading to Kachmyr, an excellent highway, upon which we travelled rapidly. We had to use no little skill in making our way through the ranks of a military caravan—its baggage carried upon camels—which was part of a detachment returning from a country camp to the city. Soon we arrived at the end of the valley of Pendjab, and climbing up a way with infinite windings, entered the passes of the Himalayas. The ascent became more and more steep. Behind us spread, like a beautiful panorama, the region we had just traversed, which seemed to sink farther and farther away from us. As the sun's last glances rested upon the tops of the mountains, our tonga came gaily out from the zigzags which the eye could still trace far down the forest-clad slope, and halted at the little city of Muré; where the families of the English functionaries come to seek shade and refreshment.

Ordinarily, one can go in a tonga from Muré to Srinagar; but at the approach of the winter season, when all Europeans desert

Kachmyr, the tonga service is suspended. I undertook my journey precisely at the time when the summer life begins to wane, and the Englishmen whom I met upon the road, returning to India, were much astonished to see me, and made vain efforts to divine the purpose of my travel to Kachmyr.

Abandoning the tonga, I hired saddle-horses —not without considerable difficulty—and evening had arrived when we started to descend from Muré, which is at an altitude of 5,000 feet. This stage of our journey had nothing playful in it. The road was torn in deep ruts by the late rains, darkness came upon us and our horses rather guessed than saw their way. When night had completely set in, a tempestuous rain surprised us in the open country, and, owing to the thick foliage of the centennarian oaks which stood on the sides of our road, we were plunged in profound darkness. That we might not lose each other, we had to continue exchanging calls from time to time. In this impenetrable obscurity we divined huge masses of rock almost above our heads, and were conscious of, on our left, a roaring torrent, the waters of which formed a cascade we could not see. During two hours we waded in the mud and the icy rain had chilled my very marrow, when we perceived in the distance a little fire, the sight of which revived our energies. But how deceitful are lights in the mountains! You believe you see the fire burning quite near to you and at once it disappears, to re-appear again, to the right, to the left, above, below you, as if it took pleasure in playing tricks upon the harassed traveller. All the time the road makes a thousand turns, and winds here and there, and the fire—which is immovable—seems to be in continual motion, the obscurity preventing you realizing that you yourself modify your direction every instant.

I had quite given up all hope of approaching this much-wished-for fire, when it appeared again, and this time so near that our horses stopped before it.

I have here to express my sincere thanks to the Englishmen for the foresight of which they gave proof in building by the road-sides the little bengalows—one-story houses for the shelter of travellers. It is true, one must not demand comfort in this kind of hotel; but this is a matter in which the traveller, broken down by fatigue, is not exacting, and he is at the summit of happiness when he finds at his disposal a clean and dry room.

The Hindus, no doubt, did not expect to see a traveller arrive at so late an hour of the night and in this season, for they had taken away the keys of the bengalow, so we had to force an entrance. I threw myself upon a bed prepared for me, composed of a pillow and blanket saturated with water, and almost at once fell asleep. At daybreak, after taking tea and some conserves, we took up our march again, now bathed in the burning rays of the sun. From time to time, we passed villages; the first in a superb narrow pass, then along the road meandering in the bosom of the mountain. We descended eventually to the river Djeloum (Jhelum), the waters of which flow gracefully, amid the rocks by which its course is obstructed, between rocky walls whose tops in many places seem almost to reach the azure skies of the Himalayas, a heaven which here shows itself remarkably pure and serene.

Toward noon we arrived at the hamlet called Tongue—situated on the bank of the river—which presents an unique array of huts that give the effect of boxes, the openings of which form a façade. Here are sold comestibles and all kinds of merchandise. The place swarms with Hindus, who bear on their foreheads the variously colored marks of their respective castes. Here, too, you see the beautiful people of Kachmyr, dressed in their long white shirts and snowy turbans. I hired here, at a good price, a Hindu cabriolet, from a Kachmyrian. This vehicle is so constructed that in order to keep one's seat in it, one must cross his legs in the Turkish fashion. The seat is so small that it will hold, at most, only two persons. The absence of any support for the back makes this mode of transportation very dangerous; nevertheless, I accepted this kind of circular table mounted on two wheels and drawn by a horse, as I was anxious to reach, as soon as possible, the end of my journey. Hardly, however, had I gone five hundred yards on it, when I seriously regretted the horse I had forsaken, so much fatigue had I to endure keeping my legs crossed and maintaining my equilibrium. Unfortunately, it was already too late.

Evening was falling when I approached the village of Hori. Exhausted by fatigue; racked by the incessant jolting; my legs feeling as if invaded by millions of ants, I had been completely incapable of enjoying the picturesque landscape spread before us as we journeyed along the Djeloum, the banks of which are bordered on one side by steep rocks and on the other by the heavily wooded slopes of mountains. In Hori I encountered a caravan of pilgrims returning from Mecca.

Thinking I was a physician and learning my haste to reach Ladak, they invited me to join them, which I promised them I would at Srinagar.

I spent an ill night, sitting up in my bed, with a lighted torch in my hand, without closing my eyes, in constant fear of the stings and bites of the scorpions and centipedes which swarm in the bengalows. I was sometimes ashamed of the fear with which those vermin inspired me; nevertheless, I could not fall asleep among them. Where, truly, in man, is the line that separates courage from cowardice? I will not boast of my bravery, but I am not a coward, yet the insurmountable fear with which those malevolent little creatures thrilled me, drove sleep from my eyelids, in spite of my extreme fatigue.

Our horses carried us into a flat valley, encircled by high mountains. Bathed as I was in the rays of the sun, it did not take me long to fall asleep in the saddle. A sudden sense of freshness penetrated and awoke me. I saw that we had already begun climbing a mountain path, in the midst of a dense forest, rifts in which occasionally opened to our admiring gaze ravishing vistas, impetuous torrents; distant mountains; cloudless heavens; a landscape, far below, of wondrous beauty. All about us were the songs of numberless brilliantly plumaged birds. We came out of the forest toward noon, descended to a little hamlet on the bank of the river, and after refreshing ourselves with a light, cold collation, continued our journey. Before starting, I went to a bazaar and tried to buy there a glass of warm milk from a Hindu, who was sitting crouched before a large cauldron full of boiling milk. How great was my surprise when he proposed to me that I should take away the whole cauldron, with its contents, assuring me that I had polluted the milk it contained! "I only want a glass of milk and not a kettle of it," I said to him.

"According to our laws," the merchant answered me, "if any one not belonging to our caste has fixed his eyes for a long time upon one of our cooking utensils, we have to wash that article thoroughly, and throw away the food it contains. You have polluted my milk and no one will drink any more of it, for not only were you not contented with fixing your eyes upon it, but you have even pointed to it with your finger."

I had indeed a long time examined his merchandise, to make sure that it was really milk, and had pointed with my finger, to the merchant, from which side I wished the milk poured out. Full of respect for the laws and customs of foreign peoples, I paid, without dispute, a rupee, the price of all the milk, which was poured in the street, though I had taken only one glass of it. This was a lesson which taught me, from now on, not to fix my eyes upon the food of the Hindus.

There is no religious belief more muddled by the numbers of ceremonious laws and commentaries prescribing its observances than the Brahminic.

While each of the other principal religions has but one inspired book, one Bible, one

Gospel, or one Koran—books from which the Hebrew, the Christian and the Musselman draw their creeds—the Brahminical Hindus possess such a great number of tomes and commentaries in folio that the wisest Brahmin has hardly had the time to peruse one-tenth of them. Leaving aside the four books of the Vedas; the Puranas—which are written in Sanscrit and composed of eighteen volumes—containing 400,000 strophes treating of law, rights, theogony, medicine, the creation and destruction of the world, etc.; the vast Shastras, which deal with mathematics, grammar, etc.; the Upa-Vedas, Upanishads, Upo-Puranas—which are explanatory of the Puranas;—and a number of other commentaries in several volumes; there still remain twelve vast books, containing the laws of Manu, the grandchild of Brahma—books dealing not only with civil and criminal law, but also the canonical rules—rules which impose upon the faithful such a considerable number of ceremonies that one is surprised into admiration of the illimitable patience the Hindus show in observance of the precepts inculcated by Saint Manu. Manu was incontestably a great legislator and a great thinker, but he has written so much that it has happened to him frequently to contradict himself in the course of a single page. The Brahmins do not take the trouble to notice that, and the poor Hindus, whose labor supports the Brahminic caste, obey servilely their clergy, whose prescriptions enjoin upon them never to touch a man who does not belong to their caste, and also absolutely prohibit a stranger from fixing his attention upon anything belonging to a Hindu. Keeping himself to the strict letter of this law, the Hindu imagines that his food is polluted when it receives a little protracted notice from the stranger.

And yet, Brahminism has been, even at the beginning of its second birth, a purely monotheistic religion, recognizing only one infinite and indivisible God. As it came to pass in all times and in all religions, the clergy took advantage of the privileged situation which places them above the ignorant multitude, and early manufactured various exterior forms of cult and certain laws, thinking they could better, in this way, influence and control the masses. Things changed soon, so far that the principle of monotheism, of which the Vedas have given such a clear conception, became confounded with, or, as it were, supplanted by an absurd and limitless series of gods and goddesses, half-gods, genii and devils, which were represented by idols, of infinite variety but all equally horrible-looking. The people, once glorious as their religion was once great and pure, now slip by degrees into complete idiocy. Hardly does their day suffice for the accomplishment of all the prescriptions of their canons. It must be said positively that the Hindus only exist to support their principal caste, the Brahmins, who have taken into their hands the temporal power which once was possessed by independent sovereigns of the people. While governing India, the Englishman does not interfere with this phase of the public life, and so the Brahmins profit by maintaining the people's hope of a better future.

The sun passed behind the summit of a

mountain, and the darkness of night in one moment overspread the magnificent landscape we were traversing. Soon the narrow valley of the Djeloum fell asleep. Our road winding along ledges of steep rocks, was instantly hidden from our sight; mountains and trees were confounded together in one dark mass, and the stars glittered in the celestial vault. We had to dismount and feel our way along the mountain side, for fear of becoming the prey of the abyss which yawned at our feet. At a late hour of the night we traversed a bridge and ascended a steep elevation leading to the bengalow Ouri, which at this height seems to enjoy complete isolation. The next day we traversed a charming region, always going along the river—at a turn of which we saw the ruins of a Sikh fortress, that seemed to remember sadly its glorious past. In a little valley, nestled amid the mountains, we found a bengalow which seemed to welcome us. In its proximity were encamped a cavalry regiment of the Maharajah of Kachmyr.

When the officers learned that I was a Russian, they invited me to share their repast. There I had the pleasure of making the acquaintance of Col. Brown, who was the first to compile a dictionary of the Afghan-pouchton language.

As I was anxious to reach, as soon as possible, the city of Srinagar, I, with little delay, continued my journey through the picturesque region lying at the foot of the mountains, after having, for a long time, followed the course of the river. Here, before our eyes, weary of the monotonous desolation of the preceding landscapes, was unfolded a charming view of a well-peopled valley, with many two-story houses surrounded by gardens and cultivated fields. A little farther on begins the celebrated valley of Kachmyr, situated behind a range of high rocks which I crossed toward evening. What a superb panorama revealed itself before my eyes, when I found myself at the last rock which separates the valley of Kachmyr from the mountainous country I had traversed. A ravishing tableau truly enchanted my sight. This valley, the limits of which are lost in the horizon, and is throughout well populated, is enshrined amid the high Himalayan mountains. At the rising and the setting of the sun, the zone of eternal snows seems a silver ring, which like a girdle surrounds this rich and delightful plateau, furrowed by numerous rivers and traversed by excellent roads.

Gardens, hills, a lake, the islands in which are occupied by constructions of pretentious style, all these cause the traveller to feel as if he had entered another world. It seems to him as though he had to go but a little farther on and there must find the Paradise of which his governess had told him so often in his childhood.

The veil of night slowly covered the valley, merging mountains, gardens and lake in one dark amplitude, pierced here and there by distant fires, resembling stars. I descended into the valley, directing myself toward the Djeloum, which has broken its way through a narrow gorge in the mountains, to unite itself with the waters of the river Ind. According to the legend, the valley was once an inland sea; a passage opened through the rocks environing it, and drained the waters away, leaving nothing more of its former character than the lake, the Djeloum and minor water-courses. The banks of the river are now lined with boat-houses, long and narrow, which the proprietors, with their families, inhabit the whole year.

From here Srinagar can be reached in one day's travel on horseback; but with a boat the journey requires a day and a half. I chose the latter mode of conveyance, and having selected a boat and bargained with its proprietor for its hire, took my seat in the bow, upon a carpet, sheltered by a sort of pent-house roof. The boat left the shore at midnight, bearing us rapidly toward Srinagar. At the stern of the bark, a Hindu prepared my tea. I went to sleep, happy in knowing my voyage was to be accomplished. The hot caress of the sun's rays penetrating beneath my little roof awakened me, and what I experienced delighted me beyond all expression. Entirely green banks; the distant outlines of mountain tops covered with snow; pretty villages which from time to time showed themselves at the mountain's foot; the crystalline sheet of water; pure and peculiarly agreeable air, which I breathed with exhilaration; the musical carols of an infinity of birds; a sky of extraordinary purity; behind me the plash of water stirred by the round-ended paddle which was wielded with ease by a superb woman (with marvellous eyes and a complexion browned by the sun), who wore an air of stately indifference: all these things together seemed to plunge me into an ecstasy, and I forgot entirely the reason for my presence on the river. In that moment I had not even a desire to reach the end of my voyage—and yet, how many privations remained for me to undergo, and dangers to encounter! I felt myself here so well content!

The boat glided rapidly and the landscape continued to unfold new beauties before my eyes, losing itself in ever new combinations with the horizon, which merged into the mountains we were passing, to become one with them. Then a new panorama would display itself, seeming to expand and flow out from the sides of the mountains, becoming more and more grand. . . . The day was almost spent and I was not yet weary of contemplating this magnificent nature, the view of which reawakened the souvenirs of childhood and youth. How beautiful were those days forever gone!

The more nearly one approaches Srinagar,

the more numerous become the villages embowered in the verdure. At the approach of our boat, some of their inhabitants came running to see us; the men in their turbans, the women in their small bonnets, both alike dressed in white gowns reaching to the ground, the children in a state of nudity which reminded one of the costumes of our first parents.

When entering the city one sees a range of barks and floating houses in which entire families reside. The tops of the far-off, snow-covered mountains were caressed by the last rays of the setting sun, when we glided between the wooden houses of Srinagar, which closely line both banks of the river. Life seems to cease here at sunset; the thousands of many-colored open boats (dunga) and palanquin-covered barks (bangla) were fastened along the beach; men and women gathered near the river, in the primitive costumes of Adam and Eve, going through their evening ablutions without feeling any embarrassment or prudery before each other, since they performed a religious rite, the importance of which is greater for them than all human prejudices.

On the 20th of October I awoke in a neat room, from which I had a gay view upon the river that was now innundated with the rays of the sun of Kachmyr. As it is not my purpose to describe here my experiences in detail, I refrain from enumerating the lovely valleys, the paradise of lakes, the enchanting islands, those historic palaces, mysterious pagodas, and coquettish villages which seem lost in vast gardens; on all sides of which rise the majestic tops of the giants of the

Himalaya, shrouded as far as the eye can see in eternal snow. I shall only note the preparations I made in view of my journey toward Thibet. I spent six days at Srinagar, making long excursions into the enchanting surroundings of the city, examining the numerous ruins which testify to the ancient prosperity of this region, and studying the strange customs of the country.

Kachmyr, as well as the other provinces attached to it, Baltistan, Ladak, etc., are vassals of England. They formerly formed part of the possessions of Randjid Sing, the Lion of the Pendjab. At his death, the English troops occupied Lahore, the capital of the Pendjab, separated Kachmyr from the rest of the empire and ceded it, under color of hereditary right and for the sum of 160,000,000 francs, to Goulab-Sing, one of the familiars of the late sovereign, conferring on him besides the title of Maharadja. At the epoch of my journey, the actual Maharadja was Pertab-Sing, the grandchild of Goulab, whose residence is Jamoo, on the southern slope of the Himalaya.

The celebrated "happy valley" of Kachmyr (eighty-five miles long by twenty-five miles wide) enjoyed glory and prosperity only under the Grand Mogul, whose court loved to taste here the sweetness of country life, in the still existent pavilions on the little island of the lake. Most of the Maharadjas of Hindustan used formerly to spend here the summer months, and to take part in the magnificent festivals given by the Grand Mogul; but times have greatly changed since, and the happy valley is to-day no more than a beggar-retreat. Aquatic plants and scum have covered the clear waters of the lake; the wild juniper has smothered all the vegetation of the islands; the palaces and pavilions retain only the souvenir of their past grandeur; earth and grass cover the buildings which are now falling in ruins. The surrounding mountains and their eternally white tops seem to be absorbed in a sullen sadness, and to nourish the hope of a better time for the disclosure of their immortal beauties. The once spiritual, beautiful and cleanly inhabitants have grown animalistic and stupid; they have become dirty and lazy; and the whip now governs them, instead of the sword.

The people of Kachmyr have so often been subject to invasions and pillages and have had so many masters, that they have now become indifferent to every thing. They pass their time near the banks of the rivers, gossiping about their neighbors; or are engaged in the painstaking work of making their celebrated shawls; or in the execution of filagree gold or silver work. The Kachmyr women are of a melancholy temperament, and an inconceivable sadness is spread upon their features. Everywhere reigns misery and uncleanness. The beautiful men and superb women of Kachmyr are dirty and in rags. The costume of the two sexes consists, winter and summer alike, of a long shirt, or gown, made of thick material and with puffed sleeves. They wear this shirt until it is completely worn out, and never is it washed, so that the white turban of the men looks like dazzling snow near their dirty shirts, which are covered all over with spittle and grease stains.

The traveller feels himself permeated with sadness at seeing the contrast between the rich and opulent nature surrounding them, and this people dressed in rags.

The capital of the country, Srinagar (City of the Sun), or, to call it by the name which is given to it here after the country, Kachmyr, is situated on the shore of the Djeloum, along which it stretches out toward the south to a distance of five kilometres and is not more than two kilometres in breadth.

Its two-story houses, inhabited by a population of 100,000 inhabitants, are built of wood and border both river banks. Everybody lives on the river, the shores of which are united by ten bridges. Terraces lead from the houses to the Djeloum, where all day long people perform their ceremonial ablutions, bathe and wash their culinary utensils, which consist of a few copper pots. Part of the inhabitants practice the Musselman religion; two-thirds are Brahminic; and there are but few Buddhists to be found among them.

It was time to make other preparations for travel before plunging into the unknown. Having purchased different kinds of conserves, wine and other things indispensable on a journey through a country so little peopled as is Thibet, I packed all my baggage in boxes; hired six carriers and an interpreter, bought a horse for my own use, and fixed my departure for the 27th of October. To cheer up my journey, I took from a good Frenchman, M. Peicheau, the wine cultivator of the Maharadja, a big dog, Pamir, who had already traversed the road with my friends, Bonvallot, Capus and Pepin, the well-known explorers. As I wished to shorten my journey by two days, I ordered my carriers to leave at dawn from the other side of the lake, which I crossed in a boat, and joined them and my horse at the foot of the mountain chain which separates the valley of Srinagar from the Sind gorge.

I shall never forget the tortures which we had to undergo in climbing almost on all fours to a mountain top, three thousand feet high. The carriers were out of breath; every moment I feared to see one tumble down the declivity with his burden, and I felt pained at seeing my poor dog, Pamir, panting and with his tongue hanging out, make two or three steps and fall to the ground exhausted. Forgetting my own fatigue, I caressed and encouraged the poor animal, who, as if understanding me, got up to make another two or three steps and fall anew to the ground.

The night had come when we reached the crest; we threw ourselves greedily upon the snow to quench our thirst; and after a short rest, started to descend through a very thick pine forest, hastening to gain the village of Haïena, at the foot of the defile, fearing the attacks of beasts of prey in the darkness.

A level and good road leads from Srinagar to Haïena, going straight northward over Ganderbal, where it turns abruptly to the east, previously keeping close to the Sind, and traversing a country with a superb vegetation, as far as Kangan. Six miles from there it approaches the village of Haïena, where I repaired by a more direct route across a pass three thousand feet high, which shortened for me both time and distance.

My first step in the unknown was marked by an incident which made all of us pass an ugly quarter of an hour. The defile of the Sind, sixty miles long, is especially noteworthy for the inhospitable hosts it contains. Among others it abounds in panthers, tigers, leopards, black bears, wolves and jackals. As though by a special misfortune, the snow had covered with its white carpet the heights of the chain, compelling those formidable, carniverous beasts to descend a little lower for shelter in their dens. We descended in silence, amid the darkness, a narrow path that wound through the centennary firs and birches, and the calm of the night was only broken by the crackling sound of our steps. Suddenly, quite near to us, a terrible howling awoke the echoes of the woods. Our small troop stopped. "A panther!" exclaimed, in a low and frightened voice, my servant. The small caravan of a dozen men stood motionless, as though riveted to the spot. Then it occurred to me that at the moment of starting on our ascent, when already feeling fatigued, I had entrusted my revolver to one of the carriers, and my Winchester rifle to another. Now I felt bitter regret for having parted with my arms, and asked in a low voice where the man was to whom I had given the rifle. The howls became more and more violent, and filled the echoes of the woods, when suddenly a dull sound was heard, like the fall of some body. A minute later we heard the noise of a struggle and a cry of agony which mingled with the fierce roars of the starved animal.

"Saaïb, take the gun," I heard some one near by. I seized feverishly the rifle, but, vain trouble, one could not see two steps before oneself. A new cry, followed by a smothered howling, indicated to me vaguely the place of the struggle, toward which I crawled, divided between the ardent desire to "kill a panther" and a horrible fear of being eaten alive. No one dared to move; only after five minutes it occurred to one of the carriers to light a match. I then remembered the fear which feline animals exhibit at the presence of fire, and ordered my men to gather two or three handfuls of brush, which I set on fire. We then saw, about ten steps from us, one of our carriers stretched out on the ground, with his limbs frightfully lacerated by the claws of a huge panther. The beast still lay upon him defiantly, holding a piece of flesh in its mouth. At its side, gaped a box of wine broken open by its fall when the carrier was torn down. Hardly did I make a movement to bring the rifle to my shoulder, when the panther raised itself, and turned toward us while dropping part of its horrible meal. One moment, it appeared about to spring upon me, then it suddenly wheeled, and rending the air with a howl, enough to freeze one's blood, jumped into the midst of the thicket and disappeared.

My coolies, whom an odious fear had all the time kept prostrated on the ground, recovered little by little from their fright. Keeping in readiness a few packages of dry grass and matches, we hastened to reach the village Haïena, leaving behind the remains of the unfortunate Hindoo, whose fate we feared sharing.

An hour later we had left the forest and entered the plain. I ordered my tent erected under a very leafy plane-tree, and had a great fire made before it, with a pile of wood, which was the only protection we could employ against the ferocious beasts whose howls continued to reach us from all directions. In the forest my dog had pressed himself against me, with his tail between his legs; but once under the tent, he suddenly recovered his watchfulness, and barked incessantly the whole night, being very careful, however, not to step outside. I spent a terrible night, rifle in hand, listening to the concert of those diabolical howlings, the echoes of which seemed to shake the defile. Some panthers approached our bivouac to answer the barking of Pamir, but dared not attack us.

I had left Srinagar at the head of eleven

carriers, four of whom had to carry so many boxes of wine, four others bore my travelling effects; one my weapons, another various utensils, and finally a last, who went errands or on reconnaissance. His name was "Chicari," which means "he who accompanies the hunter and gathers the prey." I discharged him in the morning on account of his cowardice and his profound ignorance of the country, and only retained four carriers. It was but slowly that I advanced toward the village of Gounde.

How beautiful is nature in the Sind pass, and how much is it beloved by the hunters! Besides the great fallow-deer, you meet there the hind, the stag, the mountain-sheep and an immense variety of birds, among which I want to mention above all the golden pheasant, and others of red or snow-white plumage, very large partridges and immense eagles.

The villages situated along the Sind do not shine by their dimensions. They contain, for the greatest part, not more than ten to twenty huts of an extremely miserable appearance. Their inhabitants are clad in rags. Their cattle belongs to a very small race.

I crossed the river at Sambal, and stopped near the village Gounde, where I procured relay horses. In some villages they refused to hire horses to me; I then threatened them with my whip, which at once inspired respect and obedience; my money accomplished the same end; it inspired a servile obedience—not willingness—to obey my least orders.

Stick and gold are the true sovereigns in the Orient; without them the Very Grand Mogul would not have had any preponderance.

Night began to descend, and I was in a hurry to cross the defile which separates the villages Gogangan and Sonamarg. The road is in very bad condition, and the mountains are infested by beasts of prey which in the night descend into the very villages to seek their prey. The country is delightful and very fertile; nevertheless, but few colonists venture to settle here, on account of the neighborhood of the panthers, which come to the door-yards to seize domestic animals.

At the very exit of the defile, near the village of Tchokodar, or Thajwas, the half obscurity prevailing only permitted me to distinguish two dark masses crossing the road. They were two big bears followed by a young one. I was alone with my servant (the caravan having loitered behind), so I did not like to attack them with only one rifle; but the long excursions which I had made on the mountain had strongly developed in me the sense of the hunter. To jump from my horse, shoot, and, without even verifying the result, change quickly the cartridge, was the affair of a second. One bear was about to jump on me, a second shot made it run away and disappear. Holding in my hand my loaded gun, I approached with circumspection, the one at which I had aimed, and found it laying on its flank, dead, with the little cub beside it. Another shot killed the little one, after which I went to work to take off the two superb jet-black skins.

This incident made us lose two hours, and night had completely set in when I erected my tent near Tchokodar, which I left at sunrise to gain Baltal, by following the course of the Sind river. At this place the ravishing landscape of the "golden prairie" terminates abruptly with a village of the same name (Sona, gold, and Marg, prairie). The abrupt acclivity of Zodgi-La, which we next surmounted, attains an elevation of 11,500 feet, on the other side of which the whole country assumes a severe and inhospitable character. My hunting adventures closed before reaching Baltal. From there I met on the road only wild goats. In order to hunt, I would have had to leave the grand route and to penetrate into the heart of the mountains full of mysteries. I had neither the inclination nor the time to do so, and, therefore, continued quietly my journey toward Ladak.

How violent the contrast I felt when passing from the laughing nature and beautiful population of Kachmyr to the arid and forbidding rocks and the beardless and ugly inhabitants of Ladak!

The country into which I penetrated is situated at an altitude of 11,000 to 12,000 feet. Only at Karghil the level descends to 8,000 feet.

The acclivity of Zodgi-La is very rough; one must climb up an almost perpendicular rocky wall. In certain places the road winds along upon rock ledges of only a metre in width, below which the sight drops into unfathomable abysses. May the Lord preserve the traveller from a fall! At one place, the way is upon long beams introduced into holes made in the rock, like a bridge, and covered up with earth. Brr!—At the thought that a little stone might get loose and roll down the slope of the mountain, or that a too strong oscillation of the beams could precipitate the whole structure into the abyss, and with it him who had ventured upon the perilous path, one feels like fainting more than once during this hazardous passage.

After crossing the glaciers we stopped in a valley and prepared to spend the night near a hut, a dismal place surrounded by eternal ice and snow.

From Baltal the distances are determined by means of daks, *i. e.*, postal stations for mail service. They are low huts, about seven kilometres distant from each other. A man is permanently established in each of these huts. The postal service between Kachmyr and Thibet is yet carried on in a very primitive form. The letters are enclosed in a leather bag, which is handed to the care of a carrier. The latter runs rapidly over the seven kilometres assigned to him, carrying on his back a basket which holds several of these bags, which he delivers to another carrier, who, in his turn, accomplishes his task in an identical manner. Neither rain nor snow can arrest these carriers. In this way the mail service is carried on between Kachmyr and Thibet, and *vice versa* once a week. For each course the letter-carrier is paid six annas (twenty cents); the same wages as is paid to the carriers of merchandise. This sum I also paid to every one of my servants for carrying a ten times heavier load.

It makes one's heart ache to see the pale and tired-looking figures of these carriers; but what is to be done? It is the custom of the country. The tea is brought from China by a similar system of transportation, which is rapid and inexpensive.

In the village of Montaiyan, I found again the Yarkandien caravan of pilgrims, whom I had promised to accompany on their journey. They recognized me from a distance, and asked me to examine one of their men, who had fallen sick. I found him writhing in the agonies of an intense fever. Shaking my hands as a sign of despair, I pointed to the heavens and gave them to understand that human will and science were now useless, and that God alone could save him. These people journeyed by small stages only ; I, therefore, left them and arrived in the evening at Drass, situated at the bottom of a valley near a river of the same name. Near Drass, a little fort of ancient construction, but freshly painted, stands aloof, under the guard of three Sikhs of the Maharadja's army.

At Drass, my domicile was the post-house, which is a station—and the only one—of an unique telegraph line from Srinagar to the interior of the Himalayas. From that time on, I no more had my tent put up each evening, but stopped in the caravansarais; places which, though made repulsive by their dirt, are kept warm by the enormous piles of wood burned in their fireplaces.

From Drass to Karghil the landscape is unpleasing and monotonous, if one excepts the marvellous effects of the rising and setting sun and the beautiful moonlight. Apart from these the road is wearisome and abounding with dangers. Karghil is the principal place of the district, where the governor of the country resides. Its site is quite picturesque. Two water courses, the Souron and the Wakkha, roll their noisy and turbulent waters among rocks and sunken snags of up-rooted trees, escaping from their respective defiles in the rocks, to join in forming here the river Souron, upon the banks of which stands Karghil. A little fort, garrisoned by two or three Sikhs, shows its outlines at the junction of the streams. Provided with a horse, I continued my journey at break of day, entering now the province of Ladak, or Little Thibet. I traversed a ricketty bridge, composed—like all the bridges of Kachmyr—of two long beams, the ends of which were supported upon the banks and the floor made of a layer of fagots and sticks, which imparted to the traveller, at least the illusion of a suspension bridge. Soon afterward I climbed slowly up on a little plateau, which crosses the way at a distance of two kilometres, to descend into the narrow valley of Wakkha. Here there are several villages, among which, on the left shore, is the very picturesque one called Paskium.

Here my feet trod Buddhist ground. The inhabitants are of a very simple and mild disposition, seemingly ignorant of "quarrelling." Women are very rare among them. Those of them whom I encountered were distinguished from the women I had hitherto seen in India or Kachmyr, by the air of gaiety and prosperity apparent in their countenances. How could it be otherwise, since each woman in this country has, on an average, three to five husbands, and possesses them in the most legitimate way in the world. Polyandry flourishes here. However large a family may be, there is but one woman in it. If the family does not contain already more than two husbands, a bachelor may share its advantages, for a considera-tion. The days sacred to each one of those husbands are determined in advance, and all acquit themselves of their respective duties and respect each others' rights. The men generally seem feeble, with bent backs, and do not live to old age. During my travels in Ladak, I only encountered one man so old that his hair was white.

From Karghil to the centre of Ladak, the road had a more cheerful aspect than that I had traversed before reaching Karghil, its prospect being brightened by a number of little hamlets, but trees and verdure were, unfortunately, rare.

Twenty miles from Karghil, at the end of

the defile formed by the rapid current of the Wakkha, is a little village called Chargol, in the centre of which stand three chapels, decorated with lively colors (*t'horthenes*, to give them the name they bear in Thibet). Below, near the river, are masses of rocks, in the form of long and large walls, upon which are thrown, in apparent disorder, flat stones of different colors and sizes. Upon these stones are engraved all sorts of prayers, in Ourd, Sanscrit and Thibetan, and one can even find among them inscriptions in Arabic characters. Without the knowledge of my carriers, I succeeded in taking away a few of these stones, which are now in the palace of the Trocadero.

Along the way, from Chargol, one finds frequently oblong mounds, artificial constructions. After sunrise, with fresh horses,

I resumed my journey and stopped near the "gonpa" (monastery) of Moulbek, which seems glued on the flank of an isolated rock. Below is the hamlet of Wakkha, and not far from there is to be seen another rock, of very strange form, which seems to have been placed where it stands by human hands. In one side of it is cut a Buddha several metres in height. Upon it are several cylinders, the turning of which serves for prayers. They are a sort of wooden barrel, draped with yellow or white fabrics, and are attached to vertically planted stakes. It requires only the least wind to make them turn. The person who puts up one of these cylinders no longer feels it obligatory upon him to say his prayers, for all that devout believers can ask of God is written upon the cylinders. Seen from a distance this white painted monastery, standing sharply out from the gray background of the rocks, with all these whirling, petticoated wheels, produce a strange effect in this dead country. I left my horses in the hamlet of Wakkha, and, followed by my servant, walked toward the convent, which is reached by a narrow stairway cut in the rock. At the top, I was received by a very fat lama, with a scanty, straggling beard under his chin—a common characteristic of the Thibetan people—who was very ugly, but very cordial. His costume consisted of a yellow robe and a sort of big night-cap, with projecting flaps above the ears. of the same color. He held in his hand a copper prayer-machine which, from time to time, he shook with his left hand, without at all permitting that exercise to interfere with his conversation. It was his eternal prayer, which he thus communicated to the wind, so that by this element it should be borne to Heaven. We traversed a suite of low chambers, upon the walls of which were images of Buddha, of all sizes and made of all kinds of materials, all alike covered by a thick layer of dust. Finally we reached an open terrace, from which the eyes, taking in the surrounding region, rested upon an inhospitable country, strewn with grayish rocks and traversed by only a single road, which on both sides lost itself in the horizon.

When we were seated, they brought us beer, made with hops, called here "Tchang" and brewed in the cloister. It has a tendency to rapidly produce *embonpoint* upon the monks, which is regarded as a sign of the particular favor of Heaven.

They spoke here the Thibetan language. The origin of this language is full of obscurity. One thing is certain, that a king of Thibet, a contemporary of Mohammed, undertook the creation of an universal language for all the disciples of Buddha. To this end he had simplified the Sanscrit grammar, composed an alphabet containing an infinite number of signs, and thus laid the foundations of a language the pronunciation of which is one of the easiest and the writing the most complicated. Indeed, in order to represent a sound one must employ not less than eight characters. All the modern literature of Thibet is written in this language. The pure Thibetan is only spoken in Ladak and Oriental Thibet. In all the other parts of the country are employed dialects formed by the mixture of this mother language with different idioms taken from the neighboring peoples of the various regions round about. In the ordinary life of the Thibetan, there exists always two languages, one of which is absolutely incomprehensible to the women, while the other is spoken by the entire nation; but only in the convents can be found the Thibetan language in all its purity and integrity.

The lamas much prefer the visits of Europeans to those of Musselmen, and when I asked the one who received me why this was so, he answered me: "Musselmen have no point of contact at all with our religion. Only comparatively recently, in their victorious campaign, they have converted, by force, part of the Buddhists to Islam. It requires of us great efforts to bring back those Musselmen, descendants of Buddhists, into the path of the true God. As regards the Europeans, it is quite a different affair. Not only do they profess the essential principles of monotheism, but they are, in a sense, adorers of Buddha, with almost the same rites as the lamas who inhabit Thibet. The only fault of the Christians is that after having adopted the great doctrines of Buddha, they have completely separated themselves from him, and have created for themselves a different Dalai-Lama. Our Dalai-Lama is the only one who has received the divine gift of seeing, face to face, the majesty of Buddha, and is empowered to serve as an intermediary between earth and heaven."

"Which Dalai-Lama of the Christians do you refer to?" I asked him; "we have one, the Son of God, to whom we address directly our fervent prayers, and to him alone we recur to intercede with our One and Indivisible God."

"It is not him o. whom it is a question, Sahib," he replied. "We, too, respect him, whom we reverence as son of the One and Indivisible God, but we do not see in him the Only Son, but the excellent being who was chosen among all. Buddha, indeed, has incarnated himself, with his divine nature, in the person of the sacred Issa, who, without employing fire or iron, has gone forth to propagate our true and great religion among all the world. Him whom I meant was your terrestrial Dalai-Lama; he to whom you have given the title of 'Father of the Church.' That is a great sin. May he be brought back, with the flock, who are now in a bad road," piously added the lama, giving another twirl to his prayer-machine.

I understood now that he alluded to the Pope. "You have told me that a son of Buddha, Issa, the elect among all, had spread your religion on the Earth. Who is he?" I asked.

At this question the lama's eyes opened wide; he looked at me with astonishment and pronounced some words I could not catch, murmuring in an unintelligible way. "Issa," he finally replied, "is a great prophet, one of the first after the twenty-two Buddhas. He is greater than any one of all the Dalai-Lamas, for he constitutes part of the spirituality of our Lord. It is he who has instructed you; he who brought back into the bosom of God the frivolous and wicked souls; he who made you worthy of the beneficence of the Creator, who has ordained that each being should know good and evil. His name and his acts have been chronicled in our sacred writings, and when reading how his great life passed away in the midst of an erring people, we weep for the horrible sin of the heathen who murdered him, after subjecting him to torture."

I was struck by this recital of the lama. The prophet Issa—his tortures and death—our Christian Dalai-Lama—the Buddhist recognizing Christianity—all these made me think more and more of Jesus Christ. I asked my interpreter not to lose a single word of what the lama told me.

"Where can those writings be found, and who compiled them?" I asked the monk.

"The principal scrolls — which were written in India and Nepaul, at different epochs, as the events happened—are in Lhassa; several thousands in number. In some great convents are to be found copies, which the lamas, during their sojourn in Lhassa, have made, at various times, and have then given to their cloisters as souvenirs of the period they spent with the Dalai-Lama."

"But you, yourselves; do you not possess copies of the scrolls bearing upon the prophet Issa?"

"We have not. Our convent is insignificant, and since its foundation our successive lamas have had only a few hundred manuscripts in their library. The great cloisters have several thousands of them; but they are sacred things which will not, anywhere, be shown to you."

We spoke togetner a few minutes longer, after which I went home, all the while thinking of the lama's statements. Issa, a prophet of the Buddhists! But, how could this be?

Of Jewish origin, he lived in Palestine and in Egypt; and the Gospels do not contain one word, not even the least allusion, to the part which Buddhism should have played in the education of Jesus.

I made up my mind to visit all the convents of Thibet, in the hope of gathering fuller information upon the prophet Issa, and perhaps copies of the chronicles bearing upon this subject.

We traversed the Namykala Pass, at 30,000 feet of altitude, whence we descended into the valley of the River Salinoumah. Turning southward, we gained Karbou, leaving behind us, on the opposite bank, numerous villages, among others, Chagdoom, which is at the top of a rock, an extremely imposing sight. Its houses are white and have a sort of festive look, with their two and three stories. This, by the way, is a common peculiarity of all the villages of Ladak. The eye of the European, travelling in Kachmyr, would soon lose sight of all architecture to which he had been accustomed. In Ladak, on the contrary, he would be agreeably surprised at seeing the little two and three-story houses, reminders to him of those in European provinces. Near the city of Karbou, upon two perpendicular rocks, one sees the ruins of a little town or village. A tempest and an earthquake are said to have shaken down its walls, the solidity of which seems to have been exceptional.

The next day I traversed the Fotu-La Pass, at an altitude of 13,500 feet. At its summit stands a little *t'horthene* (chapel). Thence, following the dry bed of a stream, I descended to the hamlet of Lamayure, the sudden appearance of which is a surprise to the traveller. A convent, which seems grafted on the side of the rock, or held there in some miraculous way, dominates the village. Stairs are unknown in this cloister. In order to pass from one story of it to another, ropes are used. Communication with the world outside is through a labyrinth of passages in the rock. Under the windows of the convent—which make one think of birds' nests on the face of a cliff—is a little inn, the rooms of which are little inviting. Hardly had I stretched myself on the carpet in one of them, when the monks, dressed in their yellow robes, filled the apartment, bothered me with questions as to whence I came, the purpose of my coming, where I was going, and so on, finally inviting me to come and see them.

In spite of my fatigue I accepted their invitation and set out with them, to climb up the excavated passages in the rock, which were encumbered with an infinity of prayer cylinders and wheels, which I could not but touch and set turning as I brushed past them. They are placed there that they may be so turned, saving to the passers-by the time they might otherwise lose in saying their prayers—as if their affairs were so absorbing, and their time so precious, that they could not find leisure to pray. Many pious Buddhists use for this purpose an apparatus arranged to be turned by the current of a stream. I have seen a long row of cylinders, provided with their prayer formulas, placed along a river bank, in such a way that the water kept them constantly in motion, this ingenious device freeing the proprietors from any further obligation to say prayers themselves.

I sat down on a bench in the hall, where semi-obscurity reigned. The walls were garnished with little statues of Buddha, books and prayer-wheels. The loquacious lamas began explaining to me the significance of each object.

"And those books?" I asked them; "they, no doubt, have reference to religion."

"Yes, sir. These are a few religious volumes which deal with the primary and principal rites of the life common to all. We possess several parts of the words of Buddha consecrated to the Great and Indivisible Divine Being, and to all that issued from his hands."

"Is there not, among those books, some account of the prophet Issa?"

"No, sir," answered the monk. "We only possess a few principal treatises relating to the observance of the religious rites. As for the biographies of our saints, they are collected in Lhassa. There are even great cloisters which have not had the time to procure them. Before coming to this gonpa, I was for several years in a great convent on the other side of Ladak, and have seen there thousands of books, and scrolls copied out of various books by the lamas of the monastery."

By some further interrogation I learned that the convent in question was near Leh, but my persistent inquiries had the effect of exciting the suspicions of the lamas. They showed me the way out with evident pleasure, and, regaining my room, I fell asleep—after a light lunch—leaving orders with my Hindu to inform himself in a skilful way, from some of the younger lamas of the convent, about the monastery in which their chief had lived before coming to Lamayure.

In the morning, when we set forth on our journey, the Hindu told me that he could get nothing from the lamas, who were very reticent. I will not stop to describe the life of the monks in those convents, for it is the same in all the cloisters of Ladak. I have seen the celebrated monastery of Leh—of which I shall have to speak later on—and learned there the strange existences the monks and religious people lead, which is everywhere the same. In Lamayure commences a declivity which, through a steep, narrow and sombre gorge, extends toward India.

Without having the least idea of the dangers which the descent presented, I sent my carriers in advance and started on a route, rather pleasant at the outset, which passes between the brown clay hills, but soon it produced upon me the most depressing effect, as though I was traversing a gloomy subterranean passage. Then the road came out on the flank of the mountain, above a terrible abyss. If a rider had met me, we could not possibly have passed each other, the way was so narrow. All description would fail to convey a sense of the grandeur and wild beauty of this cañon, the summit of the walls of which seemed to reach the sky. At some points it became so narrow that from my saddle I could, with my cane, touch the opposite rock. At other places, death might be fancied looking up expectantly, from the abyss, at the traveller. It was too late to dismount. In entering alone this gorge, I had not the faintest idea that I would have occasion to regret my foolish imprudence. I had not realized its character. It was simply an enormous crevasse, rent by some Titanic throe of nature, some tremendous earthquake, which had split the granite mountain. In its bottom I could just distinguish a hardly perceptible white thread, an impetuous torrent, the dull roar of which filled the defile with mysterious and impressive sounds. Far overhead extended, narrow and sinuously, a blue ribbon, the only glimpse of the celestial world that the frowning granite walls permitted to be seen. It was a thrilling pleasure, this majestic view of nature. At the same time, its rugged severity, the vastness of its proportions, the deathly silence only invaded by the ominous murmur from the depths beneath, all together filled me with an unconquerable depression. I had about eight miles in which to experience these sensations, at once sweet and painful. Then, turning to the right, our little caravan reached a small valley, almost surrounded by precipitous granite rocks, which mirrored themselves in the Indus. On the bank of the river stands the little fortress Khalsi, a celebrated fortification dating from the epoch of the Musselman invasion, by which runs the wild road from Kachmyr to Thibet.

We crossed the Indus on an almost suspended bridge which led directly to the door of the fortress, thus impossible of evasion. Rapidly we traversed the valley, then the village of Khalsi, for I was anxious to spend the night in the hamlet of Snowely, which is placed upon terraces descending to the Indus. The two following days I travelled tranquilly and without any difficulties to overcome, along the shore of the Indus, in a picturesque country—which brought me to Leh, the capital of Ladak.

While traversing the little valley of Saspoula, at a distance of several kilometres from the village of the same name, I found "*t'horthenes*" and two cloisters, above one of which floated the French flag. Later on, I learned that a French engineer had presented the flag to the monks, who displayed it simply as a decoration of their building.

I passed the night at Saspoula and certainly did not forget to visit the cloisters, seeing there for the tenth time the omnipresent dust-covered images of Buddha; the flags and banners heaped in a corner; ugly masks on the floor; books and papyrus rolls heaped together without order or care, and the inevitable abundance of prayer-wheels. The lamas demonstrated a particular pleasure in exhibiting these things, doing it with the air of shopmen displaying their goods, with very little care for the degree of interest the traveller may take in them. "We must show everything, in the hope that the sight alone of these sacred objects will force the traveller to believe in the divine grandeur of the human soul."

Respecting the prophet Issa, they gave me the same account I already had, and I learned, what I had known before, that the books which could instruct me about him were at Lhassa, and that only the great monasteries possessed some copies. I did not think any more of passing Kara-koroum, but only of finding the history of the prophet Issa, which would, perhaps, bring to light the entire life of the best of men, and complete the rather vague information which the Gospels afford us about him.

Not far from Leh, and at the entrance of the valley of the same name, our road passed near an isolated rock, on the top of which were constructed a fort—with two towers and without garrison—and a little convent named Pitak. A mountain, 10,500 feet high, protects the entrance to Thibet. There the road makes a sudden turn toward the north, in the direction of Leh, six miles from Pitak and a thousand feet higher. Immense granite mountains tower above Leh, to a height of 18,000 or 19,000 feet, their crests covered with eternal snow. The city itself, surrounded by a girdle of stunted aspen trees, rises upon successive terraces, which are dominated by an old fort and the palaces of the ancient sovereigns of Ladak. Toward evening I made my entrance into Leh, and stopped at a bengalow constructed especially for Europeans, whom the road from India brings here in the hunting season.

LADAK.

Ladak formerly was part of Great Thibet. The powerful invading forces from the north which traversed the country to conquer Kachmyr, and the wars of which Ladak was the theatre, not only reduced it to misery, but eventually subtracted it from the political domination of Lhassa, and made it the prey of one conqueror after another. The Musselmen, who sized Kachmyr and Ladak at a remote epoch, converted by force the poor inhabitants of old Thibet to the faith of Islam. The political existence of Ladak ended with the annexation of this country to Kachmyr by the sëiks, which, however, permitted the Ladakians to return to their ancient beliefs. Two-thirds of the inhabitants took advantage of this opportunity to rebuild their gonpas and take up their past life anew. Only the Baltistans remained Musselman schüttes—a sect to which the conquerors of the country had belonged. They, however, have only conserved a vague shadow of Islamism, the character of which manifests itself in their ceremonials and in the polygamy which they practice. Some lamas affirmed to me that they did not despair of one day bringing them back to the faith of their ancestors.

From the religious point of view Ladak is a dependency of Lhassa, the capital of Thibet and the place of residence of the Dalai-Lama. In Lhassa are located the principal Khoutoukhtes, or Supreme Lamas, and the Chogzots, or administrators. Politically, it is under the authority of the Maharadja of Kachmyr, who is represented there by a governor.

The inhabitants of Ladak belong to the Chinese-Touranian race, and are divided into Ladakians and Tchampas. The former lead a sedentary existence, building villages of two-story houses along the narrow valleys, are cleanly in their habits, and cultivators of the soil. They are excessively ugly; thin, with stooping figures and small heads set deep between their shoulders; their cheek bones salient, foreheads narrow, eyes black and brilliant, as are those of all the Mongol race; noses flat, mouths large and thin-lipped; and from their small chins, very thinly garnished by a few hairs, deep wrinkles extend upward fu owing their hollow cheeks. To all this, add a close-shaven head with only a little bristling fringe of hair, and you will have the general type, not alone of Ladak, but of entire Thibet.

The women are also of small stature, and have exceedingly prominent cheek bones, but seem to be of much more robust constitution. A healthy red tinges their cheeks and sympathetic smiles linger upon their lips. They have good dispositions, joyous inclinations, and are fond of laughing.

The severity of the climate and rudeness of the country, do not permit to the Ladakians much latitude in quality and colors of costume. They wear gowns of simple gray linen and coarse dull-hued clothing of their own manufacture. The pantaloons of the men only descend to their knees. People in good circumstances wear, in addition to the ordinary dress, the "choga," a sort of overcoat which is draped on the back when not wrapped around the figure. In winter they wear fur caps, with big ear flaps, and in summer cover their heads with a sort of cloth hood, the top of which dangles on one side, like a Phrygian cap. Their shoes are made of felt and covered with leather. A whole arsenal of little things hangs down from their belts, among which you will find a needle case, a knife, a pen and inkstand, a tobacco pouch, a pipe, and a diminutive specimen of the omnipresent prayer-cylinder.

The Thibetan men are generally so lazy, that if a braid of hair happens to become loose, it is not tressed up again for three months, and when once a shirt is put on the body, it is not again taken off until it falls to pieces. Their overcoats are always unclean, and, on the back, one may contemplate a long oily stripe imprinted by the braid of hair, which is carefully greased every day. They wash themselves once a year, but even then do not do so voluntarily, but because compelled by law. They emit such a terrible stench that one avoids, as much as possible, being near them.

The Thibetan women, on the contrary, are very fond of cleanliness and order. They wash themselves daily and as often as may be needful. Short and clean chemises hide their dazzling white necks. The Thibetan woman throws on her round shoulders a red jacket, the flaps of which are covered by tight pantaloons of green or red cloth, made in such a manner as to puff up and so protect the legs against the cold. She wears embroidered red half-boots, trimmed and lined with fur. A large cloth petticoat with numerous folds completes her home toilet. Her hair is arranged in thin braids, to which, by means of pins, a large piece of floating cloth is attached,—which reminds one of the head-dress so common in Italy. Underneath this sort of veil are suspended a variety of various colored pebbles, coins and pieces of metal. The ears are covered by flaps made of cloth or fur. A furred sheepskin covers the back, poor women contenting themselves with a simple plain skin of the animal, while wealthy ladies wear veritable cloaks, lined with red cloth and adorned with gold fringes.

The Ladak woman, whether walking in the streets or visiting her neighbors, always carries upon her back a conical basket, the smaller end of which is toward the ground. They fill it with the dung of horses or cows, which constitute the combustible of the country. Every woman has money of her own, and spends it for jewelry. Generally she purchases, at a small expense, large pieces of turquoise, which are added to the *bizarre* ornaments of her headdress. I have seen pieces so worn which weighed nearly five pounds. The Ladak woman occupies a social position for which she is envied by all women of the Orient. She is free and respected. With the exception of some rural work, she passes the greatest part of her time in visiting. It must, however, be added that women's gossip is here a perfectly unknown thing.

The settled population of Ladak is engaged in agriculture, but they own so little land (the share of each may amount to about eight acres) that the revenue drawn from it is insufficient to provide them with the barest necessities and does not permit them to pay taxes. Manual occupations are generally despised. Artisans and musicians form the lowest class of society. The name by which they are designated is Bem, and people are very careful not to contract any alliance with them. The hours of leisure left by rural work are spent in hunting the wild sheep of Thibet, the skins of which are highly valued in India. The poorest, *i. e.*, those who have not the means to purchase arms for hunting, hire themselves as coolies. This is also an occupation of women, who are very capable of enduring arduous toil. They are healthier than their husbands, whose laziness goes so far that, careless of cold or heat, they are capable of spending a whole night in the open air on a bed of stones rather than take the trouble to go to bed.

Polyandry (which I shall treat later more fully) causes the formation of very large families, who, in common, cultivate their jointly possessed lands, with the assistance of yaks, zos and zomos (oxen and cows). A member of a family cannot detach himself from it, and when he dies, his share reverts to the survivors in common.

They sow but little wheat and the grain is very small, owing to the severity of the climate. They also harvest barley, which they pulverize before selling. When work in the field is ended, all male inhabitants go to gather on the mountain a wild herb called "enoriota," and large thorn bushes or "dama," which are used as fuel, since combustibles are scarce in Ladak. You see there neither trees nor gardens, and only exceptionally thin clumps of willows and poplars grow on the shores of the rivers. Near the villages are also found some aspen trees ; but, on account of the unfertility of the ground, arboriculture is unknown and gardening is little successful.

The absence of wood is especially noticeable in the buildings, which are made of sun-dried bricks, or, more frequently, of stones of medium size which are agglomerated with a kind of mortar composed of clay and chopped straw. The houses of the settled inhabitants are two stories high, their fronts whitewashed, and their window-sashes painted with lively colors. The flat roof forms a terrace which is decorated with wild flowers, and here, during good weather, the inhabitants spend much of their time contemplating nature, or turning their prayer-wheels. Every dwelling-house is composed of many rooms; among them always one of superior size, the walls of which are decorated with superb fur-skins, and which is reserved for visitors. In the other rooms are beds and other furniture. Rich people possess, moreover, a special room filled with all kinds of idols, and set apart as a place of worship.

Life here is very regular. They eat anything attainable, without much choice; the principal nourishment of the Ladak people, however, being exceedingly simple. Their breakfast consists of a piece of rye bread. At dinner, they serve on the table a bowl with meal into which lukewarm water is stirred with little rods until the mixture assumes the consistency of thick paste. From this, small portions are scooped out and eaten with milk. In the evening, bread and tea are served. Meat is a superfluous luxury. Only the hunters introduce some variety in their alimentation, by eating the meat of wild sheep, eagles or pheasants, which are very common in this country.

During the day, on every excuse and opportunity, they drink "tchang," a kind of pale, unfermented beer.

If it happens that a Ladakian, mounted on a pony (such privileged people are very rare), goes to seek work in the surrounding country, he provides himself with a small stock of meal; when dinner time comes, he descends to a river or spring, mixes with water, in a wooden cup that he always has with him, some of the meal, swallows the simple refreshment and washes it down with water.

The Tchampas, or nomads, who constitute the other part of Ladak's population, are rougher, and much poorer than the settled population. They are, for the most part, hunters, who completely neglect agriculture. Although they profess the Buddhistic religion, they never frequent the cloisters unless in want of meal, which they obtain in exchange for their venison. They mostly camp in tents on the summits of the mountains, where the cold is very great. While the properly called Ladakians are peaceable, very desirous of learning, of an incarnated laziness, and are never known to tell untruth; the Tchampas, on the contrary, are very irascible, extremely lively, great liars and profess a great disdain for the convents.

Among them lives the small population of Khombas, wanderers from the vicinity of

Lhassa, who lead the miserable existence of a troupe of begging gipsies on the highways. Incapable of any work whatever, speaking a language not spoken in the country where they beg for their subsistence, they are the objects of general contempt, and are only tolerated out of pity for their deplorable condition, when hunger drives their mendicant bands to seek alms in the villages.

Polyandry, which is universally prevalent here, of course interested my curiosity. This institution is, by the way, not the outcome of Buddha's doctrines. Polyandry existed long before the advent of Buddha. It assumed considerable proportions in India, where it constituted one of the most effective means for checking the growth of a population which tends to constant increase, an economic danger which is even yet combatted by the abominable custom of killing new-born female children, which causes terrible ravages in the child-life of India. The efforts made by the English in their enactments against the suppression of the future mothers have proved futile and fruitless. Manu himself established polyandry as a law, and Buddhist preachers, who had renounced Brahminism and preached the use of opium, imported this custom into Ceylon, Thibet, Corea, and the country of the Moguls. For a long time suppressed in China, polyandry, which flourishes in Thibet and Ceylon, is also met with among the Kalmonks, between Todas in Southern India, and Nairs on the coast of Malabar. Traces of this strange constitution of the family are also to be found with the Tasmanians and the Irquois Indians in North America.

Polyandry, by the way, has even flourished in Europe, if we may believe Cæsar, who, in his *De Bello Gallico*, book V., page 17, writes: "*Uxores habent deni duodenique inter se communes, et maxime fratres cum fratribus et parentes cum liberis.*"

In view of all this it is impossible to hold any religion responsible for the existence of the institution of polyandry. In Thibet it can be explained by motives of an economical nature; the small quantity of arable land falling to the share of each inhabitant. In order to support the 1,500,000 inhabitants distributed in Thibet, upon a surface of 1,200,000 square kilometres, the Buddhists were forced to adopt polyandry. Moreover, each family is bound to enter one of its members in a religious order. The first-born is consecrated to a gonpa, which is inevitably found upon an elevation, at the entrance of every village. As soon as the child attains the age of eighteen years, he is entrusted to the caravans which pass Lhassa, where he remains from eight to fifteen years as a novice, in one of the gonpas which are near the city. There he learns to read and write, is taught the religious rites and studies the sacred parchments written in the Pali language—which formerly used to be the language of the country of Maguada, where, according to tradition, Buddha was born.

The oldest brother remaining in a family chooses a wife, who becomes common to his brothers. The choice of the bride and the nuptial ceremonies are most rudimentary. When a wife and her husband have decided upon the marriage of a son, the brother who possesses the right of choice, pays a visit to a neighboring family in which there is a marriageable daughter.

The first and second visits are spent in more or less indifferent conversations, blended with frequent libations of tchang, and on the third visit only does the young man declare his intention to take a wife. Upon this the girl is formally introduced to him. She is generally not unknown to the wooer, as, in Ladak, women never veil their faces.

A girl cannot be married without her consent. When the young man is accepted, he takes his bride to his house, and she becomes his wife and also the wife of all his brothers. A family which has an only son sends him to a woman who has no more than two or three husbands, and he offers himself to her as a fourth husband. Such an offer is seldom declined, and the young man settles in the new family.

The newly married remain with the parents of the husbands, until the young wife bears her first child. The day after that event, the grandparents of the infant make over the bulk of their fortune to the new family, and, abandoning the old home to them, seek other shelter.

Sometimes marriages are contracted between youth who have not reached a marriageable age, but in such event, the married couple are made to live apart, until they have attained and even passed the age required. An unmarried girl who becomes *enceinte*, far from being exposed to the scorn of every one, is shown the highest respect; for she is demonstrated fruitful, and men eagerly seek her in marriage. A wife has the unquestioned right of having an unlimited number of husbands and lovers. If she likes a young man, she takes him home, announces that he has been chosen by her as a "jing-tuh" (a lover), and endows him with all the personal rights of a husband, which situation is accepted by her temporarily supplanted husbands with a certain philosophic pleasure, which is the more pronounced if their wife has proved sterile during the three first years of her marriage.

They certainly have here not even a vague idea of jealousy. The Thibetan's blood is too cold to know love, which, for him, would be almost an anachronism; if indeed he were not conscious that the sentiment of the entire community would be against him, as a flagrant violator of popular usage and established rights, in restraining the freedom of the women. The selfish enjoyment of love would be, in their eyes, an unjustifiable luxury.

In case of a husband's absence, his place may be offered to a bachelor or a widower. The latter are here in the minority, since the wife generally survives her feeble husbands. Sometimes a Buddhist traveller, whom his affairs bring to the village, is chosen for this office. A husband who travels, or seeks for work in the neighboring country, at every stop takes advantage of his co-religionists' hospitality, who offer him their own wives. The husbands of a sterile woman exert themselves to find opportunities for hospitality, which may happily eventuate in a change in her condition, that they may be made happy fathers.

The wife enjoys the general esteem, is ever of a cheerful disposition, takes part in everything that is going on, goes and comes without any restriction, anywhere and everywhere she pleases, with the exception of the principal prayer-room of the monastery, entrance into which is formally prohibited to her.

Children know only their mother, and do not feel the least affection for their fathers, for the simple reason that they have so many. Without approving polyandry, I could not well blame Thibet for this institution, since without it, the population would prodigiously increase. Famine and misery would fall upon the whole nation, with all the sinister *sequellæ* of murder and theft, crimes so far absolutely unknown in the whole country.

A FESTIVAL IN A GONPA.

Leh, the capital of Ladak, is a little town of 5,000 inhabitants, who live in white, two-story houses, upon two or three streets, principally. In its centre is the square of the bazaar, where the merchants of India, China, Turkestan, Kachmyr and Thibet, come to exchange their products for the Thibetan gold. Here the natives provide themselves with cloths for themselves and their monks, and various objects of real necessity.

An old uninhabited palace rises upon a hill which dominates the town. Fronting the central square is a vast building, two stories in height, the residence of the governor of Ladak, the Vizier Souradjbal—a very amiable and universally popular Pendjaban, who has received in London the degree of Doctor of Philosophy.

To entertain me, during my sojourn in Leh, the governor arranged, on the bazaar square, a game of polo—the national sport of the Thibetans, which the English have adopted and introduced into Europe. In the evening, after the game, the people executed dances and played games before the governor's residence. Large bonfires illuminated the scene, lighting up the throng of inhabitants, who formed a great circle about the performers. The latter, in considerable numbers, disguised as animals, devils and sorcerers, jumped and contorted themselves in rhythmic dances timed to the measure of the monotonous and unpleasing music made by two long trumpets and a drum.

The infernal racket and shouting of the crowd wearied me. The performance ended with some graceful dances by Thibetan women, who spun upon their heels, swaying to and fro, and, in passing before the spectators in the windows of the residence, greeted us by the clashing together of the copper and ivory bracelets on their crossed wrists.

The next day, at an early hour, I repaired to the great Himis convent, which, a little distance from Leh, is elevated upon the top of a great rock, on a picturesque site, commanding the valley of the Indies. It is one of the principal monasteries of the country, and is maintained by the gifts of the people and the subsidies it receives from Lhassa. On the road leading to it, beyond the bridge crossing the Indus, and in the vicinity of the villages lining the way, one finds heaps of stones bearing engraved inscriptions, such as have already been described, and *t'hörthenes.* At these places, our guides were very careful to turn to the right. I wished to turn my horse to the left, but the Ladakians made him go back and led him by his halter to the right, explaining to me that such was their established usage. I found it impossible to learn the origin or reason of this custom.

Above the gonpa rises a battlemented tower, visible from a great distance. We climbed, on foot, to the level on which the edifice stands and found ourselves confronted by a large door, painted in brilliant colors, the portal of a vast two-story building enclosing a court paved with little pebbles. To the right, in one of the angles of the court, is another huge painted door, adorned with big copper rings. It is the entrance to the principal temple, which is decorated with paintings of the principal gods, and contains a great statue of Buddha and a multitude of sacred statuettes. To the left, upon a verandah, was placed an immense prayer-cylinder. All the lamas of the convent, with their chief, stood about it, when we entered the court. Below the verandah were musicians, holding long trumpets and drums.

At the right of the court were a number of doors, leading to the rooms of the lamas; all decorated with sacred paintings and provided with little prayer-barrels fancifully surmounted by black and white tridents, from the points of which floated ribbons bearing inscriptions—doubtless prayers. In the centre of the court were raised two tall masts, from the tops of which dangled tails of yaks, and long paper streamers floated, covered with religious inscriptions. All along the walls were numerous prayer-barrels, adorned with ribbons.

A profound silence reigned among the many spectators present. All awaited anxiously the commencement of a religious "mystery," which was about to be presented. We took up a position near the verandah. Almost immediately, the musicians drew from their long trumpets soft and monotonous tones, marking the time by measured beats upon an odd-looking drum, broad and shallow, upreared upon a stick planted in the ground. At the first sounds of the strange music, in which joined the voices of the lamas in a melancholy chant, the doors along the wall opened simultaneously, giving entrance to about twenty masked persons, disguised as animals, birds, devils and imaginary monsters. On their breasts they bore representations of fantastic dragons, demons and skulls, embroidered with Chinese silk of various colors. From the conical hats they wore, depended to their breasts long multicolored ribbons, covered with inscriptions. Their masks were white death's-heads. Slowly they marched about the masts, stretching out their arms from time to time and flourishing with their left hands spoon-shaped objects, the bowl portions of which were said to be fragments of human crania, with ribbons attached, having affixed to their ends human hair, which, I was assured, had been taken from scalped enemies. Their promenade, in gradually narrowing circles about the masts, soon became merely a confused jostling of each other; when the rolling of the drum grew more accentuated, the performers for an instant stopped, then started again, swinging above their heads yellow sticks, ribbon-decked, which with their right hands they brandished in menacing attitudes.

After making a salute to the chief lama, they approached the door leading to the temple, which at this instant opened, and from it another band came forth, whose heads were covered by copper masks. Their dresses were of rich materials, embroidered in various bright colors. In one hand each of them carried a small tambourine and with the other he agitated a little bell. From the rim of each tambourine depended a metallic ball, so placed that the least movement of the hand brought it in contact with the resonant tympanum, which caused a strange, continuous under-current of pulsating sound. These new performers circled several times about the court, marking the time of their dancing steps by measured thumpings of the tambourines. At the completion of each turn, they made a deafening noise with their instruments. Finally, they ran to the temple-door and ranged themselves upon the steps before it.

For a moment, there was silence. Then we saw emerge from the temple a third band of performers. Their enormous masks represented different deities, and each bore upon its forehead "the third eye." At their head marched Thlogan-Poudma-Jungnas (literally "he who was born in the lotus flower"). Another richly dressed mask marched beside him, carrying a yellow parasol covered with symbolic designs. His suite was composed of gods, in magnificent costumes; Dorje-Trolong and Sangspa-Kourpo (*i. e.*, Brahma himself), and others. These masks, as a lama sitting near me explained to us, represented six classes of beings subject to the metamorphoses; the gods, the demi-gods, men, animals, spirits and demons.

On each side of these personages, who advanced gravely, marched other masks, costumed in silks of brilliant hues and wearing on their heads golden crowns, fashioned with six lotus-like flowers on each, surmounted by a tall dart in the centre. Each of these masks carried a drum.

These disguises made three turns about the masts, to the sound of a noisy and incoherent music, and then seated themselves on the ground, around Thlogan-Pondma-

Jungnas, a god with three eyes, who gravely introduced two fingers into his mouth and emitted a shrill whistle. At this signal, young men dressed in warrior costumes—with ribbon-decked bells dangling about their legs—came with measured steps from the temple. Their heads were covered by enormous green masks, from which floated triangular red flags, and they, too, carried tambourines. Making a diabolical din, they whirled and danced about the gods seated on the ground. Two big fellows accompanying them, who were dressed in tight clown costumes, executed all kinds of grotesque contortions and acrobatic feats, by which they won plaudits and shouts of laughter from the spectators.

Another group of disguises—of which the principal features were red mitres and yellow pantaloons—came out of the temple, with bells and tambourines in their hands, and seated themselves opposite the gods, as representatives of the highest powers next to divinity. Lastly there entered upon the scene a lot of red and brown masks, with a "third eye" painted on their breasts. With those who had preceded them, they formed two long lines of dancers, who to the thrumming of their many tambourines, the measured music of the trumpets and drums, and the jingling of a myriad of bells, performed a dance, approaching and receding from each other, whirling in circles, forming by twos in a column and breaking from that formation to make new combinations, pausing occasionally to make reverent obeisance before the gods.

After a time this spectacular excitement—the noisy monotony of which began to weary me—calmed down a little; gods, demigods, kings, men and spirits got up, and followed by all the other maskers, directed themselves toward the temple door, whence issued at once, meeting them, a lot of men admirably disguised as skeletons. All those sorties were calculated and pre-arranged, and every one of them had its particular significance. The *cortége* of dancers gave way to the skeletons, who advanced with measured steps, in silence, to the masts, where they stopped and made a concerted clicking with pieces of wood hanging at their sides, simulating perfectly the rattling of dry bones and gnashing of teeth. Twice they went in a circle around the masts, marching in time to low taps on the drums, and then joined in a lugubrious religious chant. Having once more made the concerted rattling of their artificial bones and jaws, they executed some contortions painful to witness and together stopped.

Then they seized upon an image of the Enemy of Man—made of some sort of brittle paste—which had been placed at the foot of one of the masts. This they broke in pieces and scattered, and the oldest men among the spectators, rising from their places, picked up the fragments which they handed to the skeletons—an action supposed to signify that they would soon be ready to join the bony crew in the cemetery.

The chief lama, approaching me, tendered an invitation to accompany him to the principal terrace and partake of the festal "tchang;" which I accepted with pleasure, for my head was dizzy from the long spectacle.

We crossed the court and climbed a staircase—obstructed with prayer-wheels, as usual—passed two rooms where there were many images of gods, and came out upon the terrace, where I seated myself upon a bench opposite the venerable lama, whose eyes sparkled with spirit.

Three lamas brought pitchers of tchang, which they poured into small copper cups, that were offered first to the chief lama, then to me and my servants.

"Did you enjoy our little festival?" the lama asked me.

"I found it very enjoyable and am still impressed by the spectacle I have witnessed. But, to tell the truth, I never suspected for a moment that Buddhism, in these religious ceremonies, could display such a visible, not to say noisy, exterior form."

"There is no religion, the ceremonies of which are not surrounded with more theatrical forms," the lama answered. "This is a ritualistic phase which does not by any means violate the fundamental principles of Buddhism. It is a practical means for maintaining in the ignorant mass obedience to and love for the one Creator, just as a child is beguiled by toys to do the will of its parents. The ignorant mass is the child of The Father."

"But what is the meaning," I said to him, "of all those masks, costumes, bells, dances, and, generally, of this entire performance, which seems to be executed after a prescribed programme?"

"We have many similar festivals in the year," answered the lama, "and we arrange particular ones to represent 'mysteries,' susceptible of pantomimic presentation, in which each actor is allowed considerable latitude of action, in the movements and jests he likes, conforming, nevertheless, to the circumstances and to the leading idea. Our mysteries are simply pantomimes calculated to show the veneration offered to the gods, which veneration sustains and cheers the soul of man, who is prone to anxious contemplation of inevitable death and the life to come. The actors receive the dresses from the cloister and they play according to general indications, which leave them much liberty of individual action. The general effect produced is, no doubt, very beautiful, but it is a matter for the spectators themselves to divine the signification of one or another action. You, too, have recourse sometimes to similar devices, which, however, do not in the least violate the principle of monotheism."

"Pardon me," I remarked, "but this multitude of idols with which your gonpas abound, is a flagrant violation of that principle."

"As I have told you," replied the lama to my interruption, "man will always be in childhood. He sees and feels the grandeur of nature and understands everything presented to his senses, but he neither sees nor divines the Great Soul which created and animates all things. Man has always sought for tangible things. It was not possible for him to believe long in that which escaped his material senses. He has racked his brain to and means for contemplating the Creator; has endeavored to enter into direct relations with him who has done him so much good, and also, as he erroneously believes, so much evil. For this reason he began to adore every phase of nature from which he received benefits. We see a striking example of this in the ancient Egyptians, who adored animals, trees, stones, the winds and the rain. Other peoples, who were more sunk in ignorance, seeing that the results of the wind were not always beneficent, and that the rain did not inevitably bring good harvests, and that the animals were not willingly subservient to man, began to seek for direct intermediaries between themselves and the great mysterious and unfathomable power of the Creator. Therefore they made for themselves idols, which they regarded as indifferent to things concerning them, but to whose interposition in their behalf, they might always recur. From remotest antiquity to our own days, man was ever inclined only to tangible realities.

"While seeking a route to lead their feet to the Creator, the Assyrians turned their eyes toward the stars, which they contemplated without the power of attaining them. The Guebers have conserved the same belief to our days. In their nullity and spiritual blindness, men are incapable of conceiving the invisible spiritual bond which unites them to the great Divinity, and this explains why they have always sought for palpable things, which were in the domain of the senses, and by doing which they minimized the divine principle. Nevertheless, they have dared to attribute to their visible and man-made images a divine and eternal existence. We can see the same fact in Brahminism, where man, given to his inclination for exterior forms, has created, little by little, and not all at once, an army of gods and demi-gods. The Israelites may be said to have demonstrated, in the most flagrant way, the love of man for everything which is concrete. In spite of a series of striking miracles accomplished by the great Creator, who is the same for all the peoples, the Jewish people could not help making a god of metal in the very minute when their prophet Mossa spoke to them of the Creator! Buddhism has passed through the same modifications. Our great reformer, Sakya-Muni, inspired by the Supreme Judge, understood truly the one and indivisible Brahma, and forbade his disciples attempting to manufacture images in imaginary semblance of him. He had openly broken from the polytheistic Brahmins, and appreciated the purity, oneness and immortality of Brahma. The success he achieved by his teachings in making disciples among the people, brought upon him persecution by the Brahmins, who, in the creation of new gods, had found a source of personal revenue, and who, contrary to the law of God, treated the people in a despotic manner. Our first sacred teachers, to whom we give the name of buddhas—which means, learned men or saints—because the great Creator has incarnated in them, settled in different countries of the globe. As their teachings attacked especially the tyranny of the Brahmins and the misuse they made of the idea of God—of which they indeed made a veritable business—almost all the Buddhistic converts, they who followed the doctrines of those great teachers, were among the common people of China and India. Among those teachers, particular reverence is felt for the Buddha, Sakya-Muni, known in China also under the name of Fô, who lived three thousand years ago, and whose teachings brought all China back into the path of the true God ; and the Buddha, Gautama, who lived two thousand five hundred years ago, and converted almost half the Hindus to the knowledge of the impersonal, indivisible and only God, besides whom there is none.

"Buddhism is divided into many sects which, by the way, differ only in certain religious ceremonies, the basis of the doctrine being everywhere the same. The Thibetan Buddhists, who are called 'lamaists,' separated themselves from the Fô-ists fifteen hundred years ago. Until that time we had formed part of the worshippers of the Buddha, Fô-Sakya-Muni, who was the first to collect all the laws compiled by the various buddhas preceding him, when the great schism took place in the bosom of Brahmanism. Later on, a Khoutoukhte-Mongol translated into Chinese the books of the great Buddha, for which the Emperor of China rewarded him by bestowing upon him the title of 'Go-Chi—' 'Preceptor of the King!' After his death, this title was given to the Dalai-Lama of Thibet. Since that epoch, all the titularies of this position have borne the title of Go-Chi. Our religion is called the Lamaic one—from the word 'lama,' superior. It admits of two classes of monks, the red and the yellow. The former may marry, and they recognize the authority of the Bantsine, who resides in Techow Loumba, and is chief of the civil administration in Thibet. We, the yellow lamas, have taken the vow of celibacy, and our direct chief is the Dalai-Lama. This is the difference which separates the two religious orders, the respective rituals of which are identical."

"Do all perform mysteries similar to that which I have just witnessed?"

"Yes; with a few exceptions. Formerly these festivals were celebrated with very solemn pomp, but since the conquest of Ladak our convents have been, more than once, pillaged and our wealth taken away. Now we content ourselves with simple garments and bronze utensils, while in Thibet you see but golden robes and gold utensils."

"In a visit which I recently made to a gonpa, one of the lamas told me of a prophet, or, as you call him, a buddha, by the name of Issa. Could you not tell me anything about him?" I asked my interlocutor, seizing this favorable moment to start the subject which interested me so greatly.

"The name Issa is very much respected among the Buddhists," he replied, "but he is only known by the chief lamas, who have read the scrolls relating to his life. There have existed an infinite number of buddhas like Issa, and the 84,000 scrolls existing are filled brim full of details concerning each one of them. But very few persons have read the one-hundredth part of those memoirs. In conformity with established custom, every disciple or lama who visits Lhassa makes a gift of one or several copies, from the scrolls there, to the convent to which he belongs. Our gonpa, among others, possesses already a great number, which I read in my leisure hours. Among them are the memoirs of the life and acts of the Buddha Issa, who preached the same doctrine in India and among the sons of Israel, and who was put to death by the Pagans, whose descendants, later on, adopted the beliefs he spread,—and those beliefs are yours.

"The great Buddha, the soul of the Universe, is the incarnation of Brahma. He, almost always, remains immobile, containing in himself all things, being in himself the origin of all and his breath vivifying the world. He has left man to the control of his own forces, but, at certain epochs, lays aside his inaction and puts on a human form that he may, as their teacher and guide, rescue his creatures from impending destruction. In the course of his terrestrial existence in the similitude of man, Buddha creates a new world in the hearts of erring men; then he leaves the earth, to become once more an invisible being and resume his condition of perfect bliss. Three thousand years ago, Buddha incarnated in the celebrated Prince Sakya-Muni, re-affirming and propagating the doctrines taught by him in his twenty preceding incarnations. Twenty-five hundred years ago, the Great Soul of the World incarnated anew in Gautama, laying the foundation of a new world in Burmah, Siam and different islands. Soon afterward, Buddhism began to penetrate China, through the persevering efforts of the sages, who devoted themselves to the propagation of the sacred doctrine, and under Ming-Ti, of the Honi dynasty, nearly 2,050 years ago, the teachings of Sakya-Muni were adopted by the people of that country. Simultaneously with the appearance of Buddhism in China, the same doctrines began to spread among the

Israelites. It is about 2,000 years ago that the Perfect Being, awaking once more for a short time from his inaction, incarnated in the new-born child of a poor family. It was his will that this little child should enlighten the unhappy upon the life of the world to come and bring erring men back into the path of truth; showing to them, by his own example, the way they could best return to the primitive morality and purity of our race. When this sacred child attained a certain age, he was brought to India, where, until he attained to manhood, he studied the laws of the great Buddha, who dwells eternally in heaven."

"In what language are written the principal scrolls bearing upon the life of Issa?" I asked, rising from my seat, for I saw that my interesting interlocutor evidenced fatigue, and had just given a twirl to his prayer-wheel, as if to hint the closing of the conversation.

"The original scrolls brought from India to Nepaul, and from Nepaul to Thibet, relating to the life of Issa, are written in the Pali language and are actually in Lhassa; but a copy in our language—I mean the Thibetan—is in this convent."

"How is Issa looked upon in Thibet? Has he the repute of a saint?"

"The people are not even aware that he ever existed. Only the principal lamas, who know of him through having studied the scrolls in which his life is related, are familiar with his name; but, as his doctrine does not constitute a canonical part of Buddhism, and the worshippers of Issa do not recognize the authority of the Dalai-Lama, the prophet

Issa—with many others like him—is not recognized in Thibet as one of the principal saints."

"Would you commit a sin in reciting your copy of the life of Issa to a stranger?" I asked him.

"That which belongs to God," he answered me, "belongs also to man. Our duty requires us to cheerfully devote ourselves to the propagation of His doctrine. Only, I do not, at present, know where that manuscript is. If you ever visit our gonpa again, I shall take pleasure in showing it to you."

At this moment two monks entered, and uttered to the chief lama a few words unintelligible to me.

"I am called to the sacrifices. Will you kindly excuse me?" said he to me, and, with a salute, turned to the door and disappeared.

I could do no better than withdraw and lie down in the chamber which was assigned to me, and where I spent the night.

In the evening of the next day I was again in Leh—thinking of how to get back to the convent. Two days later I sent, by a messenger, to the chief lama, as presents, a watch, an alarm clock, and a thermometer. At the same time I sent the message that before leaving Ladak I would probably return to the convent, in the hope that he would permit me to see the manuscript which had been the subject of our conversation. It was now my purpose to gain Kachmyr and return from there, some time later, to Himis. But fate made a different decision for me.

In passing a mountain, on a height of which is perched the gonpa of Piatak, my horse made a false step, throwing me to the ground so violently that my right leg was broken below the knee.

It was impossible to continue my journey, I was not inclined to return to Leh; and seeking the hospitality of the gonpa of Piatak was not, from the appearance of the cloister, an enticing prospect. My best recourse would be to return to Himis, then only about half a day's journey distant, and I ordered my servants to transport me there. They bandaged my broken leg—an operation which caused me great pain—and lifted me into the saddle. One carrier walked by my side, supporting the weight of the injured member, while another led my horse. At a late hour of the evening we reached the door of the convent of Himis.

When informed of my accident, the kind monks came out to receive me and, with a wealth of extraordinary precautions of tenderness, I was carried inside, and, in one of their best rooms, installed upon an improvised bed, consisting of a mountain of soft fabrics, with the naturally-to-be-expected prayer-cylinder beside me. All this was done for me under the personal supervision of their chief lama, who, with affectionate sympathy, pressed the hand I gave him in expression of my thanks for his kindness.

In the morning, I myself bound around the injured limb little oblong pieces of wood, held by cords, to serve as splints. Then I remained perfectly quiescent and nature was not slow in her reparative work. Within two days my condition was so far improved that I could, had it been necessary, have left the gonpa and directed myself slowly toward India in search of a surgeon to complete my cure.

While a boy kept in motion the prayer-barrel near my bed, the venerable lama who ruled the convent entertained me with many interesting stories. Frequently he took from their box the alarm clock and the watch, that I might illustrate to him the process of winding them and explain to him their uses. At length, yielding to my ardent insistence, he brought me two big books, the large leaves of which were of paper yellow with age, and from them read to me the biography of Issa, which I carefully transcribed in my travelling note-book according to the translation made by the interpreter. This curious document is compiled under the form of isolated verses, which, as placed, very often had no apparent connection with, or relation to each other.

On the third day, my condition was so far improved as to permit the prosecution of my journey. Having bound up my leg as well as possible, I returned, across Kachmyr, to India; a slow journey, of twenty days, filled with intolerable pain. Thanks, however, to a litter, which a French gentleman, M. Peicheau, had kindly sent to me (my gratitude for which I take this occasion to express), and to an ukase of the Grand Vizier of the Maharajah of Kachmyr, ordering the local authorities to provide me with carriers, I reached Srinagar, and left almost immediately, being anxious to gain India before the first snows fell.

In Muré I encountered another Frenchman, Count André de Saint Phall, who was making a journey of recreation across Hindostan. During the whole course, which we made together, to Bombay, the young count demonstrated a touching solicitude for me, and sympathy for the excruciating pain I suffered from my broken leg and the fever induced by its torture. I cherish for him sincere gratitude, and shall never forget the friendly care which I received upon my arrival in Bombay from the Marquis de Morés, the Vicomte de Breteul, M. Monod, of the Comptoir d'Escompte, M. Moët, acting consul, and all the members of the very sympathetic French colony there.

During a long time I revolved in my mind

the purpose of publishing the memoirs of the life of Jesus Christ found by me in Himis, of which I have spoken, but other interests absorbed my attention and delayed it. Only now, after having passed long nights of wakefulness in the co-ordination of my notes and grouping the verses conformably to the march of the recital, imparting to the work, as a whole, a character of unity, I resolve to let this curious chronicle see the light.

THE LIFE OF SAINT ISSA.

"BEST OF THE SONS OF MEN."

I.

1. The earth trembled and the heavens wept, because of the great crime committed in the land of Israel.

2. For there was tortured and murdered the great and just Issa, in whom was manifest the soul of the Universe;

3. Which had incarnated in a simple mortal, to benefit men and destroy the evil spirit in them;

4. To lead back to peace, love and happiness, man, degraded by his sins, and recall him to the one and indivisible Creator whose mercy is infinite.

5. The merchants coming from Israel have given the following account of what has occurred:

II.

1. The people of Israel—who inhabit a fertile country producing two harvests a year and affording pasture for large herds of cattle—by their sins brought down upon themselves the anger of the Lord;

2. Who inflicted upon them terrible chastisements, taking from them their land, their cattle and their wealth. They were carried away into slavery by the rich and mighty Pharaohs who then ruled the land of Egypt.

3. The Israelites were, by the Pharaohs, treated worse than beasts, condemned to hard labor and put in irons; their bodies were covered with wounds and sores; they

were not permitted to live under a roof, and were starved to death;

4. That they might be maintained in a state of continual terror and deprived of all human resemblance;

5. And in this great calamity, the Israelites, remembering their Celestial Protector, implored his forgiveness and mercy.

6. At that period reigned in Egypt an illustrious Pharaoh, who was renowned for his many victories, immense riches, and the gigantic palaces he had erected by the labor of his slaves.

7. This Pharaoh had two sons, the younger of whom, named Mossa, had acquired much knowledge from the sages of Israel.

8. And Mossa was beloved by all in Egypt, for his kindness of heart and the pity he showed to all sufferers.

9. When Mossa saw that the Israelites, in spite of their many sufferings, had not forsaken their God, and refused to worship the gods of Egypt, created by the hands of man.

10. He also put his faith in their invisible God, who did not suffer them to betray Him, despite their ever growing weakness.

11. And the teachers among Israel animated Mossa in his zeal, and prayed of him that he would intercede with his father, Pharaoh, in favor of their co-religionists.

12. Prince Mossa went before his father, begging him to lighten the burden of the unhappy people; Pharaoh, however, became incensed with rage, and ordered that they should be tormented more than before.

13. And it came to pass that Egypt was visited by a great calamity. The plague decimated young and old, the healthy and the

SICK; and Pharaoh beheld in this the resentment of his own gods against him.

14. But Prince Mossa said to his father that it was the God of his slaves who thus interposed on behalf of his wretched people, and avenged them upon the Egyptians.

15. Thereupon, Pharaoh commanded Mossa, his son, to gather all the Israelite slaves, and lead them away, and found, at a great distance from the capital, another city where he should rule over them.

16. Then Mossa made known to the Hebrew slaves that he had obtained their freedom in the name of his and their God, the God of Israel; and with them he left the city and departed from the land of Egypt.

17. He led them back to the land which, because of their many sins, had been taken from them. There he gave them laws and

admonished them to pray always to God, the indivisible Creator, whose kindness is infinite.

18. After Prince Mossa's death, the Israelites observed rigorously his laws; and God rewarded them for the ills to which they had been subjected in Egypt.

19. Their kingdom became one of the most powerful on earth; their kings made themselves renowned for their treasures, and peace reigned in Israel.

III.

1. The glory of Israel's wealth spread over the whole earth, and the surrounding nations became envious.

2. But the Most High himself led the victorious arms of the Hebrews, and the Pagans did not dare to attack them.

3. Unfortunately, man is prone to err, and the fidelity of the Israelites to their God was not of long duration.

4. Little by little they forgot the favors he had bestowed upon them; rarely invoked his name, and sought rather protection by the magicians and sorcerers.

5. The kings and the chiefs among the people substituted their own laws for those given by Mossa; the temple of God and the observances of their ancient faith were neglected; the people addicted themselves to sensual gratifications and lost their original purity.

6. Many centuries had elapsed since their exodus from Egypt, when God bethought himself of again inflicting chastisement upon them.

7. Strangers invaded Israel, devastated

the land, destroyed the villages, and carried their inhabitants away into captivity.

8. At last came the Pagans from over the sea, from the land of Romeles. These made themselves masters of the Hebrews, and placed over them their army chiefs, who governed in the name of Cæsar.

9. They defiled the temples, forced the inhabitants to cease the worship of the indivisible God, and compelled them to sacrifice to the heathen gods.

10. They made common soldiers of those who had been men of rank; the women became their prey, and the common people, reduced to slavery, were carried away by thousands over the sea.

11. The children were slain, and soon, in the whole land, there was naught heard but weeping and lamentation.

12. In this extreme distress, the Israelites once more remembered their great God, implored his mercy and prayed for his forgiveness. Our Father, in his inexhaustible clemency, heard their prayer.

IV.

1. At that time the moment had come for the compassionate Judge to re-incarnate in a human form;

2. And the eternal Spirit, resting in a state of complete inaction and supreme bliss, awakened and separated from the eternal Being, for an undetermined period,

3. So that, in human form, He might teach man to identify himself with the Divinity and attain to eternal felicity;

4. And to show, by His example, how man can attain moral purity and free his soul from the domination of the physical senses, so that it may achieve the perfection neces sary for it to enter the Kingdom of Heaven, which is immutable and where bliss eternal reigns.

5. Soon after, a marvellous child was born in the land of Israel. God himself spoke, through the mouth of this child, of the miseries of the body and the grandeur of the soul.

6. The parents of the infant were poor people, who belonged to a family noted for great piety; who forgot the greatness of their ancestors in celebrating the name of the Creator and giving thanks to Him for the trials which He had sent upon them.

7. To reward them for adhering to the

path of truth, God blessed the first-born of this family; chose him for His elect, and sent him to sustain the fallen and comfort the afflicted.

8. The divine child, to whom the name Issa was given, commenced in his tender years to talk of the only and indivisible God, exhorting the strayed souls to repent and purify themselves from the sins of which they had become guilty.

9. People came from all parts to hear him, and marvelled at the discourses which came from his infantile mouth; and all Israel agreed that the Spirit of the Eternal dwelt in this child.

10. When Issa was thirteen years old, the age at which an Israelite is expected to marry,

11. The modest house of his industrious

parents became a meeting-place of the rich and illustrious, who were anxious to have as a son-in-law the young Issa, who was already celebrated for the edifying discourses he made in the name of the All-Powerful.

12. Then Issa secretly absented himself from his father's house; left Jerusalem, and, in a train of merchants, journeyed toward the Sindh,

13. With the object of perfecting himself in the knowledge of the word of God and the study of the laws of the great Buddhas.

V.

1. In his fourteenth year, young Issa, the Blessed One, came this side of the Sindh and settled among the Aryas, in the country beloved by God.

2. Fame spread the name of the marvellous youth along the northern Sindh, and when he came through the country of the five streams and Radjipoutan, the devotees of the god Djaïne asked him to stay among them.

3. But he left the deluded worshippers of Djaïne and went to Djagguernat, in the country of Orsis, where repose the mortal remains of Vyassa-Krishna, and where the white priests of Brahma welcomed him joyfully.

4. They taught him to read and to understand the Vedas, to cure physical ills by means of prayers, to teach and to expound the sacred Scriptures, to drive out evil desires from man and make him again in the likeness of God.

5. He spent six years in Djagguernat, in

Radjagriha, in Benares, and in other holy cities. The common people loved Issa, for he lived in peace with the Vaisyas and the Sudras, to whom he taught the Holy Scriptures.

6. But the Brahmins and the Kshatriyas told him that they were forbidden by the great Para-Brahma to come near to those who were created from his belly and his feet;*

7. That the Vaisyas might only hear the recital of the Vedas, and this only on the festal days, and

8. That the Sudras were not only forbidden to attend the reading of the Vedas, but even to look on them; for they were condemned to perpetual servitude, as slaves of the Brahmins, the Kshatriyas and even the Vaisyas.

* The Vaisyas and Sudras castes.

9. "Death alone can enfranchise them from their servitude," has said Para-Brahma. "Leave them, therefore, and come to adore with us the gods, whom you will make angry if you disobey them."

10. But Issa, disregarding their words, remained with the Sudras, preaching against the Brahmins and the Kshatriyas.

11. He declaimed strongly against man's arrogating to himself the authority to deprive his fellow-beings of their human and spiritual rights. "Verily," he said, "God has made no difference between his children, who are all alike dear to Him."

12. Issa denied the divine inspiration of the Vedas and the Puranas, for, as he taught his followers,—"One law has been given to man to guide him in his actions:

13. "Fear the Lord, thy God; bend thy

knees only before Him and bring to Him only the offerings which come from thy earnings."

14. Issa denied the Trimurti and the incarnation of Para-Brahma in Vishnu, Siva, and other gods; "for," said he:

15. "The eternal Judge, the eternal Spirit, constitutes the only and indivisible soul of the universe, and it is this soul alone which creates, contains and vivifies all.

16. "He alone has willed and created. He alone has existed from eternity, and His existence will be without end; there is no one like unto Him either in the heavens or on the earth.

17. "The great Creator has divided His power with no other being; far less with inanimate objects, as you have been taught to

believe, for He alone is omnipotent and all-sufficient.

18. "He willed, and the world was. By one divine thought, He reunited the waters and separated them from the dry land of the globe. He is the cause of the mysterious life of man, into whom He has breathed part of His divine Being.

19. "And He has put under subjection to man, the lands, the waters, the beasts and everything which He created, and which He himself preserves in immutable order, allotting to each its proper duration.

20. "The anger of God will soon break forth upon man; for he has forgotten his Creator; he has filled His temples with abominations; and he adores a multitude of creatures which God has subordinated to him;

21. "And to gain favor with images of

stone and metal, he sacrifices human beings in whom dwells part of the Spirit of the Most High;

22. "And he humiliates those who work in the sweat of their brows, to gain favor in the eyes of the idler who sitteth at a sumptuous table.

23. "Those who deprive their brothers of divine happiness will themselves be deprived of it; and the Brahmins and the Kshatriyas shall become the Sudras of the Sudras, with whom the Eternal will stay forever.

24. "In the day of judgment the Sudras and the Vaisyas will be forgiven for that they knew not the light, while God will let loose his wrath upon those who arrogated his authority."

25. The Vaisyas and the Sudras were filled with great admiration, and asked Issa how

they should pray, in order not to lose their hold upon eternal life.

26. "Pray not to idols, for they cannot hear you; hearken not to the Vedas where the truth is altered; be humble and humiliate not your fellow-man.

27. "Help the poor, support the weak, do evil to none; covet not that which ye have not and which belongs to others."

VI.

1. The white priests and the warriors,* who had learned of Issa's discourse to the Sudras, resolved upon his death, and sent their servants to find the young teacher and slay him.

2. But Issa, warned by the Sudras of his

* Brahmins and Kshatriyas.

danger, left by night Djagguernat, gained the mountain, and settled in the country of the Gautamides, where the great Buddha Sakya-Muni came to the world, among a people who worshipped the only and sublime Brahma.

3. When the just Issa had acquired the Pali language, he applied himself to the study of the sacred scrolls of the Sutras.

4. After six years of study, Issa, whom the Buddha had elected to spread his holy word, could perfectly expound the sacred scrolls.

5. He then left Nepaul and the Himalaya mountains, descended into the valley of Radjipoutan and directed his steps toward the West, everywhere preaching to the people the supreme perfection attainable by man;

6. And the good he must do to his fellow-

men, which is the sure means of speedy union with the eternal Spirit. "He who has recovered his primitive purity," said Issa, "shall die with his transgressions forgiven and have the right to contemplate the majesty of God."

7. When the divine Issa traversed the territories of the Pagans, he taught that the adoration of visible gods was contrary to natural law.

8. "For to man," said he, "it has not been given to see the image of God, and it behooves him not to make for himself a multitude of divinities in the imagined likeness of the Eternal.

9. "Moreover, it is against human conscience to have less regard for the greatness of divine purity, than for animals or works of stone or metal made by the hands of man.

10. "The eternal Lawgiver is One; there are no other Gods than He; He has parted the world with none, nor had He any counsellor.

11. "Even as a father shows kindness toward his children, so will God judge men after death, in conformity with His merciful laws. He will never humiliate his child by casting his soul for chastisement into the body of a beast.

12. "The heavenly laws," said the Creator, through the mouth of Issa, "are opposed to the immolation of human sacrifices to a statue or an animal; for I, the God, have sacrificed to man all the animals and all that the world contains.

13. "Everything has been sacrificed to man, who is directly and intimately united to me, his Father; therefore, shall the man be

severely judged and punished, by my law, who causes the sacrifice of my children.

14. "Man is naught before the eternal Judge; as the animal is before man.

15. "Therefore, I say unto you, leave your idols and perform not ceremonies which separate you from your Father and bind you to the priests, from whom heaven has turned away.

16. "For it is they who have led you away from the true God, and by superstitions and cruelty perverted the spirit and made you blind to the knowledge of the truth."

VII.

1. The words of Issa spread among the Pagans, through whose country he passed, and the inhabitants abandoned their idols.

2. Seeing which, the priests demanded of him who thus glorified the name of the true God, that he should, in the presence of the people, prove the charges he made against them, and demonstrate the vanity of their idols.

3. And Issa answered them: "If your idols, or the animals you worship, really possess the supernatural powers you claim, let them strike me with a thunder-bolt before you!"

4. "Why dost not thou perform a miracle," replied the priests, "and let thy God confound ours, if He is greater than they?"

5. But Issa said: "The miracles of our God have been wrought from the first day when the universe was created; and are performed every day and every moment; whoso

sees them not is deprived of one of the most beautiful gifts of life.

6. "And it is not on inanimate objects of stone, metal or wood that He will let His anger fall, but on the men who worship them, and who, therefore, for their salvation, must destroy the idols they have made.

7. "Even as a stone and a grain of sand, which are naught before man, await patiently their use by Him,

8. "In like manner, man, who is naught before God, must await in resignation His pleasure for a manifestation of His favor.

9. "But woe to you! ye adversaries of men, if it is not the favor you await, but rather the wrath of the Most High; woe to you, if you demand that He attest His power by a miracle!

10. "For it is not the idols which He will

destroy in His wrath, but those by whom they were created; their hearts will be the prey of an eternal fire and their flesh shall be given to the beasts of prey.

11. "God will drive away the contaminated animals from His flocks; but will take to Himself those who strayed because they knew not the heavenly part within them."

12. When the Pagans saw that the power of their priests was naught, they put faith in the words of Issa. Fearing the anger of the true God, they broke their idols to pieces and caused their priests to flee from among them.

13. Issa furthermore taught the Pagans that they should not endeavor to see the eternal Spirit with their eyes; but to perceive Him with their hearts, and make

themselves worthy of His favors by the purity of their souls.

14. "Not only," he said to them, "must ye refrain from offering human sacrifices, but ye may not lay on the altar any creature to which life has been given, for all things created are for man.

15. "Withhold not from your neighbor his just due, for this would be like stealing from him what he had earned in the sweat of his brow.

16. "Deceive none, that ye may not yourselves be deceived; seek to justify yourselves before the last judgment, for then it will be too late.

17. "Be not given to debauchery, for it is a violation of the law of God.

18. "That you may attain to supreme bliss ye must not only purify yourselves, but

must also guide others into the path that will enable them to regain their primitive innocence."

VIII.

1. The countries round about were filled with the renown of Issa's preachings, and when he came unto Persia, the priests grew afraid and forbade the people hearing him;

2. Nevertheless, the villages received him with joy, and the people hearkened intently to his words, which, being seen by the priests, caused them to order that he should be arrested and brought before their High Priest, who asked him:

3. "Of what new God dost thou speak? Knowest thou not, unfortunate man that thou art! that Saint Zoroaster is the only Just

One, to whom alone was vouchsafed the honor of receiving revelations from the Most High;

4. "By whose command the angels compiled His Word in laws for the governance of His people, which were given to Zoroaster in Paradise?

5. "Who, then, art thou, who darest to utter blasphemies against our God and sow doubt in the hearts of believers?"

6. And Issa said to them: "I preach no new God, but our celestial Father, who has existed before the beginning and will exist until after the end.

7. "Of Him I have spoken to the people, who—even as innocent children—are incapable of comprehending God by their own intelligence, or fathoming the sublimity of the divine Spirit;

8. "But, as the new-born child in the night recognizes the mother's breast, so your people, held in the darkness of error by your pernicious doctrines and religious ceremonies, have recognized instinctively their Father, in the Father whose prophet I am.

9. "The eternal Being says to your people, by my mouth, 'Ye shall not adore the sun, for it is but a part of the universe which I have created for man;

10. "It rises to warm you during your work; it sets to accord to you the rest that I have ordained.

11. "To me only ye owe all that ye possess, all that surrounds you and that is above and below you.'"

12. "But," said the priests, "how could the people live according to your rules if they had no teachers?"

13. Whereupon Issa answered: "So long as they had no priests, they were governed by the natural law and conserved the simplicity of their souls;

14. "Their souls were in God and to commune with the Father they had not to have recourse to the intermediation of idols, or animals, or fire, as taught by you.

15. "Ye pretend that man must adore the sun, and the Genii of Good and Evil. But I say unto you that your doctrine is pernicious. The sun does not act spontaneously, but by the will of the invisible Creator, who has given to it being."

16. "Who, then, has caused that this star lights the day, warms man at his work and vivifies the seeds sown in the ground?"

17. "The eternal Spirit is the soul of everything animate, and you commit a great

sin in dividing Him into the Spirit of Evil and the Spirit of Good, for there is no God other than the God of Good.

18. "And He, like to the father of a family, does only good to His children, to whom He forgives their transgressions if they repent of them.

19. "And the Spirit of Evil dwells upon earth, in the hearts of those who turn the children of God away from the right path.

20. "Therefore, I say unto you; Fear the day of judgment, for God will inflict a terrible chastisement upon all those who have led His children astray and beguiled them with superstitions and errors;

21. "Upon those who have blinded them who saw; who have brought contagion to the well; who have taught the worship of

those things which God made to be subject to man, or to aid him in his works.

22. "Your doctrine is the fruit of your error in seeking to bring near to you the God of Truth, by creating for yourselves false gods."

23. When the Magi heard these words, they feared to themselves do him harm, but at night, when the whole city slept, they brought him outside the walls and left him on the highway, in the hope that he would not fail to become the prey of wild beasts.

24. But, protected by the Lord our God, Saint Issa continued on his way, without accident.

IX.

1. Issa—whom the Creator had selected to recall to the worship of the true God, men

sunk in sin—was twenty-nine years old when he arrived in the land of Israel.

2. Since the departure therefrom of Issa, the Pagans had caused the Israelites to endure more atrocious sufferings than before, and they were filled with despair.

3. Many among them had begun to neglect the laws of their God and those of Mossa, in the hope of winning the favor of their brutal conquerors.

4. But Issa, notwithstanding their unhappy condition, exhorted his countrymen not to despair, because the day of their redemption from the yoke of sin was near, and he himself, by his example, confirmed their faith in the God of their fathers.

5. "Children, yield not yourselves to despair," said the celestial Father to them, through the mouth of Issa, "for I have heard

your lamentations, and your cries have reached my ears.

6. "Weep not, oh, my beloved sons! for your griefs have touched the heart of your Father and He has forgiven you, as He forgave your ancestors.

7. "Forsake not your families to plunge into debauchery; stain not the nobility of your souls; adore not idols which cannot but remain deaf to your supplications.

8. "Fill my temple with your hope and your patience, and do not adjure the religion of your forefathers, for I have guided them and bestowed upon them of my beneficence.

9. "Lift up those who are fallen; feed the hungry and help the sick, that ye may be altogether pure and just in the day of the last judgment which I prepare for you."

10. The Israelites came in multitudes to

listen to Issa's words; and they asked him where they should thank their Heavenly Father, since their enemies had demolished their temples and robbed them of their sacred vessels.

11. Issa told them that God cared not for temples erected by human hands, but that human hearts were the true temples of God.

12. "Enter into your temple, into your heart; illuminate it with good thoughts, with patience and the unshakeable faith which you owe to your Father.

13. "And your sacred vessels! they are your hands and your eyes. Look to do that which is agreeable to God, for in doing good to your fellow-men, you perform a ceremony that embellishes the temple wherein abideth Him who has created you.

14. "For God has created you in His own image, innocent, with pure souls, and hearts filled with kindness and not made for the planning of evil, but to be the sanctuaries of love and justice.

15. "Therefore, I say unto you, soil not your hearts with evil, for in them the Eternal Being abides.

16. "When ye do works of devotion and love, let them be with full hearts, and see that the motives of your actions be not hopes of gain or self-interest;

17. For actions, so impelled, will not bring you nearer to salvation, but lead to a state of moral degradation wherein theft, lying and murder pass for generous deeds."

X.

1. Issa went from one city to another,

strengthening by the word of God the courage of the Israelites, who were near to succumbing under their weight of woe, and thousands of the people followed him to hear his teachings.

2. But the chiefs of the cities were afraid of him and they informed the principal governor, residing in Jerusalem, that a man called Issa had arrived in the country, who by his sermons had arrayed the people against the authorities, and that multitudes, listening assiduously to him, neglected their labor; and, they added, he said that in a short time they would be free of their invader rulers.

3. Then Pilate, the Governor of Jerusalem, gave orders that they should lay hold of the preacher Issa and bring him before the judges. In order, however, not to excite the

anger of the populace, Pilate directed that he should be judged by the priests and scribes, the Hebrew elders, in their temple.

4. Meanwhile, Issa, continuing his preachings, arrived at Jerusalem, and the people, who already knew his fame, having learned of his coming, went out to meet him.

5. They greeted him respectfully and opened to him the doors of their temple, to hear from his mouth what he had said in other cities of Israel.

6. And Issa said to them: "The human race perishes, because of the lack of faith; for the darkness and the tempest have caused the flock to go astray and they have lost their shepherds.

7. "But the tempests do not rage forever and the darkness will not hide the light eternally; soon the sky will become serene,

the celestial light will again overspread the earth, and the strayed flock will re-unite around their shepherd.

8. "Wander not in the darkness, seeking the way, lest ye fall into the ditch ; but gather together, sustain one another, put your faith in your God and wait for the first glimmer of light to re-appear.

9. "He who sustains his neighbor, sustains himself; and he who protects his family, protects all his people and his country.

10. "For, be assured that the day is near when you will be delivered from the darkness; you will be re-united into one family and your enemy will tremble with fear, he who is ignorant of the favor of the great God."

11. The priests and the elders who heard him, filled with admiration for his language,

asked him if it was true that he had sought to raise the people against the authorities of the country, as had been reported to the governor Pilate.

12. "Can one raise against estrayed men, to whom darkness has hidden their road and their door?" answered Issa. "I have but forewarned the unhappy, as I do here in this temple, that they should no longer advance on the dark road, for an abyss opens before their feet.

13. "The power of this earth is not of long duration and is subject to numberless changes. It would be of no avail for a man to rise in revolution against it, for one phase of it always succeeds another, and it is thus that it will go on until the extinction of human life.

14. "But do you not see that the powerful,

and the rich, sow among the children of Israel a spirit of rebellion against the eternal power of Heaven?"

15. Then the elders asked him: "Who art thou, and from what country hast thou come to us? We have not formerly heard thee spoken of and do not even know thy name!"

16. "I am an Israelite," answered Issa; "and on the day of my birth have seen the walls of Jerusalem, and have heard the sobs of my brothers reduced to slavery, and the lamentations of my sisters carried away by the Pagans;

17. "And my soul was afflicted when I saw that my brethren had forgotten the true God. When a child I left my father's house to go and settle among other people.

18. "But, having heard it said that my brethren suffered even greater miseries now,

I have come back to the land of my fathers, to recall my brethren to the faith of their ancestors, which teaches us patience upon earth in order to attain the perfect and supreme bliss above."

19. Then the wise old men put to him again this question: "We are told that thou disownest the laws of Mossa, and that thou teachest the people to forsake the temple of God?"

20. Whereupon Issa: "One does not demolish that which has been given by our Heavenly Father, and which has been destroyed by sinners. I have but enjoined the people to purify the heart of all stains, for it is the veritable temple of God.

21. "As regards the laws of Mossa, I have endeavored to re-establish them in the hearts of men; and I say unto you that ye ignore

their true meaning, for it is not vengeance but pardon which they teach. Their sense has been perverted."

XI.

1. When the priests and the elders heard Issa, they decided among themselves not to give judgment against him, for he had done no harm to any one, and, presenting themselves before Pilate—who was made Governor of Jerusalem by the Pagan king of the country of Romeles—they spake to him thus:

2. "We have seen the man whom thou chargest with inciting our people to revolt; we have heard his discourses and know that he is our countryman;

3. "But the chiefs of the cities have made to you false reports, for he is a just man, who

teaches the people the word of God. After interrogating him, we have allowed him to go in peace."

4. The governor thereupon became very angry, and sent his disguised spies to keep watch upon Issa and report to the authorities the least word he addressed to the people.

5. In the meantime, the holy Issa continued to visit the neighboring cities and preach the true way of the Lord, enjoining the Hebrews patience and promising them speedy deliverance.

6. And all the time great numbers of the people followed him wherever he went, and many did not leave him at all, but attached themselves to him and served him.

7. And Issa said: "Put not your faith in miracles performed by the hands of men, for He who rules nature is alone capable of do-

ing supernatural things, while man is impotent to arrest the wrath of the winds or cause the rain to fall.

8. "One miracle, however, is within the power of man to accomplish. It is, when his heart is filled with sincere faith, he resolves to root out from his mind all evil promptings and desires, and when, in order to attain this end, he ceases to walk the path of iniquity.

9. "All the things done without God are only gross errors, illusions and seductions, serving but to show how much the heart of the doer is full of presumption, falsehood and impurity.

10. "Put not your faith in oracles. God alone knows the future. He who has recourse to the diviners soils the temple of his heart and shows his lack of faith in his Creator.

11. "Belief in the diviners and their miracles destroys the innate simplicity of man and his childlike purity. An infernal power takes hold of him who so errs, and forces him to commit various sins and give himself to the worship of idols.

12. "But the Lord our God, to whom none can be equalled, is one omnipotent, omniscient and omnipresent; He alone possesses all wisdom and all light.

13. "To Him ye must address yourselves, to be comforted in your afflictions, aided in your works, healed in your sickness and whoso asks of Him, shall not ask in vain.

14. "The secrets of nature are in the hands of God, for the whole world, before it was made manifest, existed in the bosom of the divine thought, and has become material and visible by the will of the Most High.

15. "When ye pray to him, become again like little children, for ye know neither the past, nor the present, nor the future, and God is the Lord of Time."

XII.

1. "Just man," said to him the disguised spies of the Governor of Jerusalem, "tell us if we must continue to do the will of Cæsar, or expect our near deliverance?"

2. And Issa, who recognized the questioners as the apostate spies sent to follow him, replied to them: "I have not told you that you would be delivered from Cæsar; it is the soul sunk in error which will gain its deliverance.

3. "There cannot be a family without a head, and there cannot be order in a people

without a Cæsar, whom ye should implicitly obey, as he will be held to answer for his acts before the Supreme Tribunal."

4. "Does Cæsar possess a divine right?" the spies asked him again; "and is he the best of mortals?"

5. "There is no one 'the best' among human beings; but there are many bad, who —even as the sick need physicians—require the care of those chosen for that mission, in which must be used the means given by the sacred law of our Heavenly Father;

6. "Mercy and justice are the high prerogatives of Cæsar, and his name will be illustrious if he exercises them.

7. "But he who acts otherwise, who transcends the limits of power he has over those under his rule, and even goes so far as to put their lives in danger, offends the great Judge

and derogates from his own dignity in the eyes of men."

8. Upon this, an old woman who had approached the group, to better hear Issa, was pushed aside by one of the disguised men, who placed himself before her.

9. Then said Issa: "It is not good for a son to push away his mother, that he may occupy the place which belongs to her. Whoso doth not respect his mother—the most sacred being after his God—is unworthy of the name of son.

10. "Hearken to what I say to you: Respect woman; for in her we see the mother of the universe, and all the truth of divine creation is to come through her.

11. "She is the fount of everything good and beautiful, as she is also the germ of life and death. Upon her man depends in all his

existence, for she is his moral and natural support in his labors.

12. "In pain and suffering she brings you forth; in the sweat of her brow she watches over your growth, and until her death you cause her greatest anxieties. Bless her and adore her, for she is your only friend and support on earth.

13. "Respect her; defend her. In so doing you will gain for yourself her love; you will find favor before God, and for her sake many sins will be remitted to you.

14. "Love your wives and respect them, for they will be the mothers of to-morrow and later the grandmothers of a whole nation.

15. "Be submissive to the wife; her love ennobles man, softens his hardened heart,

tames the wild beast in him and changes it to a lamb.

16. "Wife and mother are the priceless treasures which God has given to you. They are the most beautiful ornaments of the universe, and from them will be born all who will inhabit the world.

17. "Even as the Lord of Hosts separated the light from the darkness, and the dry land from the waters, so does woman possess the divine gift of calling forth out of man's evil nature all the good that is in him.

18. "Therefore I say unto you, after God, to woman must belong your best thoughts, for she is the divine temple where you will most easily obtain perfect happiness.

19. "Draw from this temple your moral force. There you will forget your sorrows

and your failures, and recover the love necessary to aid your fellow-men.

20. "Suffer her not to be humiliated, for by humiliating her you humiliate yourselves, and lose the sentiment of love, without which nothing can exist here on earth.

21. "Protect your wife, that she may protect you—you and all your household. All that you do for your mothers, your wives, for a widow, or for any other woman in distress, you will do for your God."

XIII.

1. Thus Saint Issa taught the people of Israel for three years, in every city and every village, on the highways and in the fields, and all he said came to pass.

2. All this time the disguised spies of the

governor Pilate observed him closely, but heard nothing to sustain the accusations formerly made against Issa by the chiefs of the cities.

3. But Saint Issa's growing popularity did not allow Pilate to rest. He feared that Issa would be instrumental in bringing about a revolution culminating in his elevation to the sovereignty, and, therefore, ordered the spies to make charges against him.

4. Then soldiers were sent to arrest him, and they cast him into a subterranean dungeon, where he was subjected to all kinds of tortures, to compel him to accuse himself, so that he might be put to death.

5. The Saint, thinking only of the perfect bliss of his brethren, endured all those torments with resignation to the will of the Creator.

6. The servants of Pilate continued to torture him, and he was reduced to a state of extreme weakness; but God was with him and did not permit him to die at their hands.

7. When the principal priests and wise elders learned of the sufferings which their Saint endured, they went to Pilate, begging him to liberate Issa, so that he might attend the great festival which was near at hand.

8. But this the governor refused. Then they asked him that Issa should be brought before the elders' council, so that he might be condemned, or acquitted, before the festival, and to this Pilate agreed.

9. On the following day the governor assembled the principal chiefs, priests, elders and judges, for the purpose of judging Issa.

10. The Saint was brought from his prison. They made him sit before the governor,

between two robbers, who were to be judged at the same time with Issa, so as to show the people he was not the only one to be condemned.

11. And Pilate, addressing himself to Issa, said, "Is it true, Oh! Man; that thou incitest the populace against the authorities, with the purpose of thyself becoming King of Israel?"

12. Issa replied, "One does not become king by one's own purpose thereto. They have told you an untruth when you were informed that I was inciting the people to revolution. I have only preached of the King of Heaven, and it was Him whom I told the people to worship.

13. "For the sons of Israel have lost their original innocence and unless they return to worship the true God they will be sacrificed and their temple will fall in ruins.

14. "The worldly power upholds order in the land; I told them not to forget this. I said to them, 'Live in conformity with your situation and refrain from disturbing public order;' and, at the same time, I exhorted them to remember that disorder reigned in their own hearts and spirits

15. "Therefore, the King of Heaven has punished them, and has destroyed their nationality and taken from them their national kings, 'but,' I added, 'if you will be resigned to your fate, as a reward the Kingdom of Heaven will be yours."

16. At this moment the witnesses were introduced; one of whom deposed thus: "Thou hast said to the people that in comparison with the power of the king who would soon liberate the Israelites from the

yoke of the heathen, the worldly authorities amounted to nothing."

17. "Blessings upon thee!" said Issa. "For thou hast spoken the truth! The King of Heaven is greater and more powerful than the laws of man and His kingdom surpasses the kingdoms of this earth.

18. "And the time is not far off, when Israel, obedient to the will of God, will throw off its yoke of sin; for it has been written that a forerunner would appear to announce the deliverance of the people, and that he would re-unite them in one family."

19. Thereupon the governor said to the judges: "Have you heard this? The Israelite Issa acknowledges the crime of which he is accused. Judge him, then, according to your laws and pass upon him condemnation to death."

20. "We cannot condemn him," replied the priests and the ancients. "As thou hast heard, he spoke of the King of Heaven, and he has preached nothing which constitutes insubordination against the law."

21. Thereupon the governor called a witness who had been bribed by his master, Pilate, to betray Issa, and this man said to Issa: "Is it not true that thou hast represented thyself as a King of Israel, when thou didst say that He who reigns in Heaven sent thee to prepare His people?"

22. But Issa blessed the man and answered: "Thou wilt find mercy, for what thou hast said did not come out from thine own heart." Then, turning to the governor he said: "Why dost thou lower thy dignity and teach thy inferiors to tell falsehood, when,

without doing so, it is in thy power to condemn an innocent man?"

23. When Pilate heard his words, he became greatly enraged and ordered that Issa be condemned to death, and that the two robbers should be declared guiltless.

24. The judges, after consulting among themselves, said to Pilate: "We cannot consent to take this great sin upon us,—to condemn an innocent man and liberate malefactors. It would be against our laws.

25. "Act thyself, then, as thou seest fit." Thereupon the priests and elders walked out, and washed their hands in a sacred vessel, and said: "We are innocent of the blood of this righteous man."

XIV.

1. By order of the governor, the soldiers seized Issa and the two robbers, and led them to the place of execution, where they were nailed upon the crosses erected for them.

2. All day long the bodies of Issa and the two robbers hung upon the crosses, bleeding, guarded by the soldiers. The people stood all around and the relatives of the executed prayed and wept.

3. When the sun went down, Issa's tortures ended. He lost consciousness and his soul disengaged itself from the body, to reunite with God.

4. Thus ended the terrestrial existence of the reflection of the eternal Spirit under the

form of a man who had saved hardened sinners and comforted the afflicted.

5. Meanwhile, Pilate was afraid for what he had done, and ordered the body of the Saint to be given to his relatives, who put it in a tomb near to the place of execution. Great numbers of persons came to visit the tomb, and the air was filled with their wailings and lamentations.

6. Three days later, the governor sent his soldiers to remove Issa's body and bury it in some other place, for he feared a rebellion among the people.

7. The next day, when the people came to the tomb, they found it open and empty, the body of Issa being gone. Thereupon, the rumor spread that the Supreme Judge had sent His angels from Heaven, to remove the

mortal remains of the saint in whom part of the divine Spirit had lived on earth.

8. When Pilate learned of this rumor, he grew angry and prohibited, under penalty of death, the naming of Issa, or praying for him to the Lord.

9. But the people, nevertheless, continued to weep over Issa's death and to glorify their master; wherefore, many were carried into captivity, subjected to torture and put to death.

10. And the disciples of Saint Issa departed from the land of Israel and went in all directions, to the heathen, preaching that they should abandon their gross errors, think of the salvation of their souls and earn the perfect bliss which awaits human beings in the immaterial world, full of glory, where the

great Creator abides in all his immaculate and perfect majesty.

11. The heathen, their kings, and their warriors, listened to the preachers, abandoned their erroneous beliefs and forsook their priests and their idols, to celebrate the praises of the most wise Creator of the Universe, the King of Kings, whose heart is filled with infinite mercy

RESUMÉ.

In reading the account of the life of Issa (Jesus Christ), one is struck, on the one hand by the resemblance of certain principal passages to accounts in the Old and New Testaments; and, on the other, by the not less remarkable contradictions which occasionally occur between the Buddhistic version and Hebraic and Christian records.

To explain this, it is necessary to remember the epochs when the facts were consigned to writing.

We have been taught, from our childhood, that the Pentateuch was written by Moses himself, but the careful researches of modern scholars have demonstrated conclusively, that at the time of Moses, and even much later, there existed in the country bathed by the Mediterranean, no other writing than the hieroglyphics in Egypt and the cuniform inscriptions, found nowadays in the excavations of Babylon. We know, however, that the alphabet and parchment were known in China and India long before Moses.

Let me cite a few proofs of this statement. We learn from the sacred books of "the religion of the wise" that the alphabet was invented in China in 2800 by Fou-si, who was the first emperor of China to embrace this religion, the ritual and exterior forms of which he himself arranged. Yao, the fourth of the Chinese emperors, who is said to have belonged to this faith, published moral and civil laws, and, in 2228, compiled a penal code. The fifth emperor, Soune, proclaimed in the year of his accession to the throne that "the religion of the wise" should thenceforth be the recognized religion of the State, and, in 2282, compiled new penal laws. His laws, modified by the Emperor Vou-vange,—founder of the dynasty of the Tcheou in 1122,—are those in existence to-day, and known under the name of "Changements."

We also know that the doctrine of the Buddha Fô, whose true name was Sakya-Muni, was written upon parchment. Fô-ism began to spread in China about 260 years before Jesus Christ. In 206, an emperor of the Tsine dynasty, who was anxious to learn Buddhism, sent to India for a Buddhist by the name of Silifan, and the Emperor Ming-Ti, of the Hagne dynasty, sent, a year before Christ's birth, to India for the sacred books written by the Buddha Sakya-Muni—the founder of the Buddhistic doctrine, who lived about 1200 before Christ.

The doctrine of the Buddha Gauthama or Gothama, who lived 600 years before Jesus Christ, was written in the Pali language upon parchment. At that epoch there existed already in India about 84,000 Buddhistic manuscripts, the compilation of which required a considerable number of years.

At the time when the Chinese and the Hindus possessed already a very rich written literature, the less fortunate or more ignorant peoples who had no alphabet, transmitted their histories from mouth to mouth, and from generation to generation. Owing to the unreliability of human memory, historical facts, embellished by Oriental imagination, soon degenerated into fabulous legends, which, in the course of time, were collected, and by the unknown compilers entitled "The Five Books of Moses." As these legends ascribe to the Hebrew legislator extraordinary divine powers which enabled him to perform miracles in the presence of Pharaoh, the claim that he was an Israelite may as well have been legendary rather than historical.

The Hindu chroniclers, on the contrary, owing to their knowledge of an alphabet, were enabled to commit carefully to writing, not mere legends, but the recitals of recently occurred facts within their own knowledge, or the accounts brought to them by merchants who came from foreign countries.

It must be remembered, in this connection, that—in antiquity as in our own days—the whole public life of the Orient was concentrated in the bazaars. There the news of foreign events was brought by the merchant-caravans and sought by the dervishes, who found, in their recitals in the temples and public places, a means of subsistence. When the merchants returned home from a journey, they generally related fully during the first days after their arrival, all they had seen or heard abroad. Such have been the customs of the Orient, from time immemorial, and are to-day.

The commerce of India with Egypt and, later, with Europe, was carried on by way of Jerusalem, where, as far back as the time of King Solomon, the Hindu caravans brought precious metals and other materials for the construction of the temple. From Europe, merchandise was brought to Jerusalem by sea, and there unloaded in a port, which is now occupied by the city of Jaffa. The chronicles in question were compiled before, during and after the time of Jesus Christ.

During his sojourn in India, in the quality of a simple student come to learn the Brahminical and Buddhistic laws, no special attention whatever was paid to his life. When, however, a little later, the first accounts of the events in Israel reached India, the chroniclers, after committing to writing that which they were told about the prophet, Issa,—*viz.*, that he had for his following a whole people, weary of the yoke of their masters, and that he was crucified by order of Pilate, remembered that this same Issa had only recently sojourned in their midst, and that, an Israelite by birth, he had come to study among them, after which he had returned to his country. They conceived a lively interest for the man who had grown so rapidly under their eyes, and began to investigate his birth, his past and all the details concerning his existence.

The two manuscripts, from which the lama of the convent Himis read to me all that had a bearing upon Jesus, are compilations from divers copies written in the Thibetan language, translations of scrolls belonging to the library of Lhassa and brought, about two hundred years after Christ, from India, Nepaul and Maghada, to a convent on Mount Marbour, near the city of Lhassa, now the residence of the Dalai-Lama.

These scrolls were written in Pali, which certain lamas study even now, so as to be able to translate it into the Thibetan.

The chroniclers were Buddhists belonging to the sect of the Buddha Gothama.

The details concerning Jesus, given in the chronicles, are disconnected and mingled with accounts of other contemporaneous events to which they bear no relation.

The manuscripts relate to us, first of all,—according to the accounts given by merchants arriving from Judea in the same year when the death of Jesus occurred—that a just man by the name of Issa, an Israelite, in spite of his being acquitted twice by the judges as being a man of God, was nevertheless put to death by the order of the Pagan governor, Pilate, who feared that he might take advantage of his great popularity to re-establish the kingdom of Israel and expel from the country its conquerors.

Then follow rather incoherent communications regarding the preachings of Jesus among the Guebers and other heathens.

They seem to have been written during the first years following the death of Jesus, in whose career a lively and growing interest is shown.

One of these accounts, communicated by a merchant, refers to the origin of Jesus and his family; another tells of the expulsion of his partisans and the persecutions they had to suffer.

Only at the end of the second volume is found the first categorical affirmation of the chronicler. He says there that Issa was a man blessed by God and the best of all; that it was he in whom the great Brahma had elected to incarnate when, at a period fixed by destiny, his spirit was required to, for a time, separate from the Supreme Being.

After telling that Issa descended from poor Israelite parents, the chronicler makes a little digression, for the purpose of explaining, according to ancient accounts, who were those sons of Israel.

I have arranged all the fragments concerning the life of Issa in chronological order and have taken pains to impress upon them the character of unity, in which they were absolutely lacking.

I leave it to the *savans*, the philosophers and the theologians to search into the causes for the contradictions which may be found between the "Life of Issa" which I lay before the public and the accounts of the Gospels. But I trust that everybody will agree with me in assuming that the version which I present to the public, one compiled three or four years after the death of Jesus, from the accounts of eye-witnesses and contemporaries, has much more probability of being in conformity with truth than the accounts of the Gospels, the composition of which was effected at different epochs and at periods much posterior to the occurrence of the events.

Before speaking of the life of Jesus, I must say a few words on the history of Moses, who, according to the so-far most accredited legend, was an Israelite. In this respect the legend is contradicted by the Buddhists. We learn from the outset that Moses was an Egyptian prince, the son of a Pharaoh, and that he only was taught by learned Israelites. I believe that if this important point is carefully examined, it must be admitted that the Buddhist author may be right.

It is not my intent to argue against the Biblical legend concerning the origin of Moses, but I think everyone reading it must share my conviction that Moses could not have been a simple Israelite. His education was rather that of a king's son, and it is difficult to believe that a child introduced by chance into the palace should have been made an equal with the son of the sovereign. The rigor with which the Egyptians treated their slaves by no means attests the mildness of their character. A foundling certainly would not have been made the companion of the sons of a Pharaoh, but would be placed among his servants. Add to this the caste spirit so strictly observed in ancient Egypt, a most salient point, which is certainly calculated to raise doubts as to the truth of the Scriptural story.

And it is difficult to suppose that Moses had not received a complete education. How otherwise could his great legislative work, his broad views, his high administrative qualities be satisfactorily explained?

And now comes another question: Why should he, a prince, have attached himself to the Israelites? The answer seems to me very simple. It is known that in ancient, as well as in modern times, discussions were often raised as to which of two brothers should succeed to the father's throne. Why not admit this hypothesis, *viz.*, that Mossa, or Moses, having an elder brother whose existence forbade him to think of occupying the throne of Egypt, contemplated founding a distinct kingdom.

It might very well be that, in view of this end, he tried to attach himself to the Israelites, whose firmness of faith as well as physical strength he had occasion to admire. We know, indeed, that the Israelites of Egypt had no resemblance whatever to their descendants as regards physical constitution. The granite blocks which were handled by them in building the palaces and pyramids are still in place to testify to this fact. In the same way I explain to myself the history of the miracles which he is said to have performed before Pharaoh.

Although there are no definite arguments for denying the miracles which Moses might have performed in the name of God before Pharaoh, I think it is not difficult to realize that the Buddhistic statement sounds more probable than the Scriptural gloss. The pestilence, the small-pox or the cholera must, indeed, have caused enormous ravages among the dense population of Egypt, at an epoch when there existed yet but very rudimentary ideas about hygiene and where, consequently, such diseases must have rapidly assumed frightful virulence.

In view of Pharaoh's fright at the disasters which befell Egypt, Moses' keen wit might well have suggested to him to explain the strange and terrifying occurrences, to his father, by the intervention of the God of Israel in behalf of his chosen people.

Moses was here afforded an excellent opportunity to deliver the Israelites from their slavery and have them pass under his own domination.

In obedience to Pharaoh's will—according to the Buddhistic version—Moses led the Israelites outside the walls of the city; but, instead of building a new city within reach of the capital, as he was ordered, he left with them the Egyptian territory. Pharaoh's indignation on learning of this infringement of his commands by Moses, can easily be imagined. And so he gave the order to his soldiers to pursue the fugitives. The geographical disposition of the region suggests at once that Moses during his flight must have moved by the side of the mountains and entered Arabia by the way over the Isthmus which is now cut by the Suez Canal.

Pharaoh, on the contrary, pursued, with his troops, a straight line to the Red Sea; then, in order to overtake the Israelites, who had already gained the opposite shore, he sought to take advantage of the ebb of the sea in the Gulf, which is formed by the coast and the Isthmus, and caused his soldiers to wade through the ford. But the length of the passage proved much greater than he had expected; so that the flood-tide set in when the Egyptian host was half way across, and, of the army thus overwhelmed by the returning waves, none escaped death.

This fact, so simple in itself, has in the course of the centuries been transformed by the Israelites into a religious legend, they seeing in it a divine intervention in their behalf and a punishment which their God inflicted on their persecutors. There is, moreover, reason to believe that Moses himself saw the occurrence in this light. This, however, is a thesis which I shall try to develop in a forthcoming work.

The Buddhistic chronicle then describes the grandeur and the downfall of the kingdom of Israel, and its conquest by the foreign nations who reduced the inhabitants to slavery.

The calamities which befell the Israelites,

and the afflictions that thenceforth embittered their days were, according to the chronicler, more than sufficient reasons that God, pitying his people and desirous of coming to their aid, should descend on earth in the person of a prophet, in order to lead them back to the path of righteousness.

Thus the state of things in that epoch justified the belief that the coming of Jesus was signalized, imminent, necessary.

This explains why the Buddhistic traditions could maintain that the eternal Spirit separated from the eternal Being and incarnated in the child of a pious and once illustrious family.

Doubtless the Buddhists, in common with the Evangelists, meant to convey by this that the child belonged to the royal house of David; but the text in the Gospels, according to which "the child was born from the Holy Spirit," admits of two interpretations, while according to Buddha's doctrine, which is more in conformity with the laws of nature, the spirit has but incarnated in a child already born, whom God blessed and chose for the accomplishment of His mission on earth.

The birth of Jesus is followed by a long gap in the traditions of the Evangelists, who either from ignorance or neglect, fail to tell us anything definite about his childhood, youth or education. They commence the history of Jesus with his first sermon, *i. e.*, at the epoch, when thirty years of age, he returns to his country.

All the Evangelists tell us concerning the infancy of Jesus is marked by the lack of precision: "And the child grew, and waxed strong in spirit, filled with wisdom; and the grace of God was upon him," says one of the sacred authors (Luke 2, 40), and another: "And the child grew, and waxed strong in spirit, and was in the deserts till the day of his shewing unto Israel." (Luke 1, 80.)

As the Evangelists compiled their writings a long time after the death of Jesus, it is presumable that they committed to writing only those accounts of the principal events in the life of Jesus which happened to come to their knowledge.

The Buddhists, on the contrary, who compiled their chronicles soon after the Passion occurred, and were able to collect the surest information about everything that interested them, give us a complete and very detailed description of the life of Jesus.

In those unhappy times, when the struggle

for existence seems to have destroyed all thought of God, the people of Israel suffered the double oppression of the ambitious Herod and the despotic and avaricious Romans. Then, as now, the Hebrews put all their hopes in Providence, whom they expected, would send them an inspired man, who should deliver them from all their physical and moral afflictions. The time passed, however, and no one took the initiative in a revolt against the tyranny of the rulers.

In that era of hope and despair, the people of Israel completely forgot that there lived among them a poor Israelite who was a direct descendant from their King David. This poor man married a young girl who gave birth to a miraculous child.

The Hebrews, true to their traditions of devotion and respect for the race of their kings, upon learning of this event went in great numbers to congratulate the happy father and see the child. It is evident that Herod was informed of this occurrence. He feared that this infant, once grown to manhood, might avail himself of his prospective popularity to re-conquer the throne of his ancestors. He sent out his men to seize the child, which the Israelites endeavored to hide from the wrath of the king, who then ordered the abominable massacre of the children, hoping that Jesus would perish in this vast human hecatomb. But Joseph's family had warning of the impending danger, and took refuge in Egypt.

A short time afterward, they returned to their native country. The child had grown during those journeyings, in which his life was more than once exposed to danger.

Formerly, as now, the Oriental Israelites commenced the instruction of their children at the age of five or six years. Compelled to constantly hide him from the murderous King Herod, the parents of Jesus could not allow their son to go out, and he, no doubt, spent all his time in studying the sacred Scriptures, so that his knowledge was sufficiently beyond what would naturally have been expected of a boy of his age to greatly astonish the elders of Israel. He had in his thirteenth year attained an age when, according to Jewish law, the boy becomes an adult, has the right to marry, and incurs obligations for the discharge of the religious duties of a man.

There exists still, in our times, among the Israelites, an ancient religious custom that fixes the majority of a youth at the accomplished thirteenth year. From this epoch the youth becomes a member of the congregation and enjoys all the rights of an adult. Hence, his marriage at this age is regarded as having legal force, and is even required in the tropical countries. In Europe, however, owing to the influence of local laws and to nature, which does not contribute here so powerfully as in warm climates to the physical development, this custom is no more in force and has lost all its former importance.

The royal lineage of Jesus, his rare intelligence and his learning, caused him to be looked upon as an excellent match, and the wealthiest and most respected Hebrews would fain have had him for a son-in-law, just as even nowadays the Israelites are very desirous of the honor of marrying their daughters to the sons of Rabbis or scholars.

But the meditative youth, whose mind was far above anything corporeal, and possessed by the thirst for knowledge, stealthily left his home and joined the caravans going to India.

It stands to reason that Jesus Christ should have thought, primarily, of going to India, first, because at that epoch Egypt formed part of the Roman possessions; secondly, and principally, because a very active commercial exchange with India had made common report in Judea of the majestic character and unsurpassed richness of the arts and sciences in this marvellous country, to which even now the aspirations of all civilized peoples are directed.

Here the Evangelists once more lose the thread of the terrestrial life of Jesus. Luke says he "was in the deserts till the day of his shewing unto Israel" (Luke I. 80), which clearly demonstrates that nobody knew where the holy youth was until his sudden re-appearance sixteen years later.

Arrived in India, this land of marvels, Jesus began to frequent the temples of the Djainites.

There exists until to-day, on the peninsula of Hindustan, a sectarian cult under the name of Djainism. It forms a kind of connecting link between Buddhism and Brahminism, and preaches the destruction of all other beliefs, which, it declares, are corroded by falsehood. It dates from the seventh century before Jesus Christ and its name is derived from the word "djain" (conqueror), which was assumed by its founders as expressive of its destined triumph over its rivals.

In sympathetic admiration for the spirit of the young man, the Djainites asked him to stay with them; but Jesus left them to settle in Djagguernat, where he devoted himself to the study of treatises on religion, philosophy, etc. Djagguernat is one of the chief sacred cities of Brahmins, and, at the time of Christ, was of great religious importance. According to tradition, the ashes of the illustrious Brahmin, Krishna, who lived in 1580 B. C., are preserved there, in the hollow of a tree, near a magnificent temple, to which thousands make pilgrimage every year. Krishna collected and put in order the Vedas, which he divided into four books—Richt, Jagour, Saman and Artafan;—in commemoration of which great work he received the name of Vyasa (he who collected and divided the Vedas), and he also compiled the Vedanta and eighteen Puranas, which contain 400,000 stanzas.

In Djagguernat is also found a very precious library of Sanscrit books and religious manuscripts.

Jesus spent there six years in studying the language of the country and the Sanscrit, which enabled him to absorb the religious doctrines, philosophy, medicine and mathematics. He found much to blame in Brahminical laws and usages, and publicly joined issue with the Brahmins, who in vain endeavored to convince him of the sacred character of their established customs. Jesus, among other things, deemed it extremely unjust that the laborer should be oppressed and despised, and that he should not only be robbed of hope of future happiness, but also be denied the right to hear the religious services. He, therefore, began preaching to the Sudras, the lowest caste of slaves, telling them that, according to their own laws, God is the Father of all men; that all which exists, exists only through Him; that, before Him, all men are equal, and that the Brahmins had obscured the great principle of monotheism by misinterpreting Brahma's own words, and laying excessive stress upon observance of the exterior ceremonials of the cult.

Here are the words in which, according to the doctrine of the Brahmins, God Himself speaks to the angels: "I have been from eternity, and shall continue to be eternally. I am the first cause of everything that exists in the East and in the West, in the North and in the South, above and below, in heaven and in hell. I am older than all things. I am the Spirit and the Creation of the universe and also its Creator. I am all-powerful; I am the God of the Gods, the King of the

Kings; I am Para-Brahma, the great soul of the universe."

After the world appeared by the will of Para-Brahma, God created human beings, whom he divided into four classes, according to their colors: white (Brahmins), red (Kshatriyas), yellow (Vaisyas), and black (Sudras). Brahma drew the first from his own mouth, and gave them for their *appanage* the government of the world, the care of teaching men the laws, of curing and judging them. Therefore do the Brahmins occupy only the offices of priests and preachers, are expounders of the Vedas, and must practice celibacy.

The second caste of Kshatriyas issued from the hand of Brahma. He made of them warriors, entrusting them with the care of defending society. All the kings, princes, captains, governors and military men belong to this caste, which lives on the best terms with the Brahmins, since they cannot subsist without each other, and the peace of the country depends on the alliance of the lights and the sword, of Brahma's temple and the royal throne.

The Vaisyas, who constitute the third caste, issued from Brahma's belly. They are destined to cultivate the ground, raise cattle, carry on commerce and practice all kinds of trades in order to feed the Brahmins and the Kshatriyas. Only on holidays are they authorized to enter the temple and listen to the recital of the Vedas; at all other times they must attend to their business.

The lowest caste, that of the black ones, or Sudras, issued from the feet of Brahma to be the humble servants and slaves of the three preceding castes. They are interdicted from attending the reading of the Vedas at any time; their touch contaminates a Brahmin, Kshatriya, or even a Vaisya who comes in contact with them. They are wretched creatures, deprived of all human rights; they cannot even look at the members of the other castes, nor defend themselves, nor, when sick, receive the attendance of a physician. Death alone can deliver the Sudra from a life of servitude; and even then, freedom can only be attained under the condition that, during his whole life, he shall have served diligently and without complaint some member of the privileged classes. Then only it is promised that the soul of the Sudra shall, after death, be raised to a superior caste.

If a Sudra has been lacking in obedience to a member of the privileged classes, or has in any way brought their disfavor upon himself, he sinks to the rank of a pariah, who is banished from all cities and villages and is the object of general contempt, as an abject being who can only perform the lowest kind of work.

The same punishment may also fall upon members of another caste; these, however, may, through repentance, fasting and other trials, re-habilitate themselves in their former caste; while the unfortunate Sudra, once expelled from his, has lost it forever.

From what has been said above, it is easy to explain why the Vaisyas and Sudras were animated with adoration for Jesus, who, in spite of the threats of the Brahmins and Kshatriyas, never forsook those poor people.

In his sermons Jesus not only censured the system by which man was robbed of his right to be considered as a human being, while an ape or a piece of marble or metal was paid divine worship, but he attacked the very life of Brahminism, its system of gods, its doctrine and its "trimurti" (trinity), the angular stone of this religion.

Para-Brahma is represented with three faces on a single head. This is the "trimurti" (trinity), composed of Brahma (creator), Vishnu (conservator), and Siva (destroyer).

Here is the origin of the trimurti:—

In the beginning, Para-Brahma created the waters and threw into them the seed of procreation, which transformed itself into a brilliant egg, wherein Brahma's image was reflected. Millions of years had passed when Brahma split the egg in two halves, of which the upper one became the heaven, the lower one, the earth. Then Brahma descended to the earth under the shape of a child, established himself upon a lotus flower, absorbed himself in his own contemplation and put to himself the question: "Who will attend to the conservation of what I have created?" "I," came the answer from his mouth under the appearance of a flame. And Brahma gave to this word the name, "Vishnu," that is to say, "he who preserves." Then Brahma divided his being into two halves, the one male, the other female, the active and the passive principles, the union of which produced Siva, "the destroyer."

These are the attributes of the trimurti; Brahma, creative principle; Vishnu, preservative wisdom; Siva, destructive wrath of justice. Brahma is the substance from which everything was made; Vishnu, space wherein everything lives; and Siva, time that annihilates all things.

Brahma is the face which vivifies all; Vishnu, the water which sustains the forces of the creatures; Siva, the fire which breaks the bond that unites all objects. Brahma is the past; Vishnu, the present; Siva, the future. Each part of the trimurti possesses, moreover, a wife. The wife of Brahma is Sarasvati, goddess of wisdom; that of Vishnu, Lakshmi, goddess of virtue, and Siva's spouse is Kali, goddess of death, the universal destroyer.

Of this last union were born, Ganesa, the elephant-headed god of wisdom, and Indra, the god of the firmament, both chiefs of inferior divinities, the number of which, if all the objects of adoration of the Hindus be included, amounts to three hundred millions.

Vishnu has descended eight times upon the earth, incarnating in a fish in order to save the Vedas from the deluge, in a tortoise, a dwarf, a wild boar, a lion, in Rama, a king's son, in Krishna and in Buddha. He will come a ninth time under the form of a rider mounted on a white horse in order to destroy death and sin.

Jesus denied the existence of all these hierarchic absurdities of gods, which darken the great principle of monotheism.

When the Brahmins saw that Jesus, who, instead of becoming one of their party, as they had hoped, turned out to be their adversary, and that the people began to embrace his doctrine, they resolved to kill him: but his servants, who were greatly attached to him, forewarned him of the threatening danger, and he took refuge in the mountains of Nepaul. At this epoch, Buddhism had taken deep root in this country. It was a kind of schism, remarkable by its moral principles and ideas on the nature of the divinity—ideas which brought men closer to nature and to one another.

Sakya-Muni, the founder of this sect, was born fifteen hundred years before Jesus Christ, at Kapila, the capital of his father's kingdom, near Nepaul, in the Himalayas. He belonged to the race of the Gotamides, and to the ancient family of the Sakyas. From his infancy he evinced a lively interest in religion, and, contrary to his father's wishes, leaving his palace with all its luxury, began at once to preach against the Brahmins, for the purification of their doctrines. He died at Kouçinagara, surrounded by many faithful disciples. His body was burned, and his ashes, divided into several parts, were distributed between the cities, which, on account of his new doctrine, had renounced Brahminism.

According to the Buddhistic doctrine, the Creator reposes normally in a state of perfect inaction, which is disturbed by nothing and which he only leaves at certain destiny-determined epochs, in order to create terrestrial buddhas. To this end the Spirit disengages itself from the sovereign Creator, incarnates in a buddha and stays for some time on the earth, where he creates Bodhisattvas (masters),* whose mission it is to preach the

* *Sanscrit*:—" He whose essence (sattva) has become intelligence (bhodi)," those who need but one more incarnation to become perfect buddhas, *i. e.*, to be entitled to Nirvâna.

divine word and to found new churches of believers to whom they will give laws, and for whom they will institute a new religious order according to the traditions of Buddhism.

A terrestrial buddha is, in a certain way, a reflection of the sovereign creative Buddha, with whom he unites after the termination of his terrestrial existence. In like manner do the Bodhisattvas, as a reward for their labors and the privations they undergo, receive eternal bliss and enjoy a rest which nothing can disturb.

Jesus sojourned six years among the Buddhists, where he found the principle of monotheism still pure. Arrived at the age of twenty-six years, he remembered his fatherland, which was then oppressed by a foreign yoke. On his way homeward, he preached against idol-worship, human sacrifice, and other errors of faith, admonishing the people to recognize and adore God, the Father of all beings, to whom all are alike dear, the master as well as the slave; for they all are his children, to whom he has given this beautiful universe for a common heritage. The sermons of Jesus often made a profound impression upon the peoples among whom he came, and he was exposed to all sorts of dangers provoked by the clergy, but was saved by the very idolators who, only the preceding day, had offered their children as sacrifices to their idols.

While passing through Persia, Jesus almost caused a revolution among the adorers of Zoroaster's doctrine. Nevertheless, the priests refrained from killing him, out of fear of the peoples' vengeance. They resorted to artifice, and led him out of town at night, with the hope that he might be devoured by wild beasts. Jesus escaped this peril and arrived safe and sound in the country of Israel.

It must be remarked here that the Orientals, amidst their sometimes so picturesque misery, and in the ocean of depravation in which they slumber, always have, under the influence of their priests and teachers, a pronounced inclination for learning and understand easily good common sense explications. It happened to me more than once that, by using simple words of truth, I appealed to the conscience of a thief or some otherwise intractable person. These people, moved by a sentiment of innate honesty,—which the clergy for personal reasons of their own, tried by all means to stifle—soon became again very honest and had only contempt for those who had abused their confidence.

By the virtue of a mere word of truth, the whole of India, with its 300,000,000 of idols, could be made a vast Christian country; but . . . . . this beautiful project would, no doubt, be antagonized by certain Christians who, similar to those priests of whom I have spoken before, speculate upon the ignorance of the people to make themselves rich.

According to St. Luke, Jesus was about thirty years of age when he began preaching to the Israelites. According to the Buddhistic chroniclers, Jesus's teachings in Judea began in his twenty-ninth year. All his sermons which are not mentioned by the Evangelists, but have been preserved by the Buddhists, are remarkable for their character of divine grandeur. The fame of the new prophet spread rapidly in the country, and Jerusalem awaited with impatience his arrival. When he came near the holy city, its inhabitants went out to meet him, and led him in triumph to the temple; all of which is in agreement with Christian tradition. The chiefs and elders who heard him were filled with admiration for his sermons, and were happy to see the beneficent impression which his words exercised upon the populace. All these remarkble sermons of Jesus are full of sublime sentiments.

Pilate, the governor of the country, however, did not look upon the matter in the same light. Eager agents notified him that Jesus announced the near coming of a new kingdom, the re-establishment of the throne of Israel, and that he suffered himself to be called the Son of God, sent to bring back courage in Israel, for he, the King of Judea, would soon ascend the throne of his ancestors.

I do not purpose attributing to Jesus the *rôle* of a revolutionary, but it seems to me very probable that Jesus wrought up the people with a view to re-establish the throne to which he had a just claim. Divinely inspired, and, at the same time, convinced of the legitimacy of his pretentions, Jesus preached the spiritual union of the people in order that a political union might result.

Pilate, who felt alarmed over these rumors, called together the priests and the elders of the people and ordered them to interdict Jesus from preaching in public, and even to condemn him in the temple under the charge of apostasy. This was the best means for

Pilate to rid himself of a dangerous man, whose royal origin he knew and whose popularity was constantly increasing.

It must be said in this connection that the Israelites, far from persecuting Jesus, recognized in him the descendant of the illustrious dynasty of David, and made him the object of their secret hopes, a fact which is evident from the very Gospels which tell that Jesus preached freely in the temple, in the presence of the elders, who could have interdicted him not only the entrance to the temple, but also his preachings.

Upon the order of Pilate the Sanhedrim met and cited Jesus to appear before its tribunal. As the result of the inquiry, the members of the Sanhedrim informed Pilate that his suspicions were without any foundation whatever; that Jesus preached a religious, and not a political, propaganda; that he was expounding the Divine word, and that he claimed to have come not to overthrow, but to re-establish the laws of Moses. The Buddhistic record does but confirm this sympathy, which unquestionably existed between the young preacher, Jesus, and the elders of the people of Israel; hence their answer: "We do not judge a just one."

Pilate felt not at all assured, and continued seeking an occasion to hale Jesus before a new tribunal, as regular as the former. To this end he caused him to be followed by spies, and finally ordered his arrest.

If we may believe the Evangelists, it was the Pharisees who sought the life of Jesus, while the Buddhistic record most positively declares that Pilate alone can be held responsible for his execution. This version is evidently much more probable than the account of the Evangelists. The conquerors of Judea could not long tolerate the presence of a man who announced to the people a speedy deliverance from their yoke. The popularity of Jesus having commenced to disturb Pilate's mind, it is to be supposed that he sent after the young preacher spies, with the order to take note of all his words and acts. Moreover, the servants of the Roman governor, as true "agents provocateurs," endeavored by means of artful questions put to Jesus, to draw from him some imprudent words under color of which Pilate might proceed against him. If the preachings of Jesus had been offensive to the Hebrew priests and scribes, all they needed to do was simply to command the people not to hear and follow him, and to forbid him entrance into the temple. But the Evangelists tell us that Jesus enjoyed great popularity among the Israelites and full liberty in the temples, where Pharisees and scribes discussed with him.

In order to find a valid excuse for condemning him, Pilate had him tortured so as to extort from him a confession of high treason.

But, contrary to the rule that the innocent, overcome by their pain, will confess anything to escape the unendurable agonies inflicted upon them, Jesus made no admission of guilt. Pilate, seeing that the usual tortures were powerless to accomplish the desired result, commanded the executioners to proceed to the last extreme of their diabolic cruelties, meaning to compass the death ot Jesus by the complete exhaustion of his forces. Jesus, however, fortifying his endurance by the power of his will and zeal for his righteous cause—which was also that of his people and of God—was unconquerable by all the refinements of cruelty inflicted upon him by his executioners.

The infliction of "the question" upon Jesus evoked much feeling among the elders, and they resolved to interfere in his behalf; formally demanding of Pilate that he should be liberated before the Passover.

When their request was denied by Pilate they resolved to petition that Jesus should be brought to trial before the Sanhedrim, by whom they did not doubt his acquittal—which was ardently desired by the people—would be ordained.

In the eyes of the priests, Jesus was a saint, belonging to the family of David; and his unjust detention, or—what was still more to be dreaded—his condemnation, would have saddened the celebration of the great national festival of the Israelites.

They therefore prayed Pilate that the trial of Jesus should take place before the Passover, and to this he acceded. But he ordered that two thieves should be tried at the same time with Jesus, thinking to, in this way, minimize in the eyes of the people, the importance of the fact that the life of an innocent man was being put in jeopardy before the tribunal; and, by not allowing Jesus to be condemned alone, blind the populace to the unjust pre-arrangement of his condemnation.

The accusation against Jesus was founded upon the depositions of the bribed witnesses.

During the trial, Pilate availed himself of

perversions of Jesus' words concerning the heavenly kingdom, to sustain the charges made against him. He counted, it seems, upon the effect produced by the answers of Jesus, as well as upon his own authority, to influence the members of the tribunal against examining too minutely the details of the case, and to procure from them the sentence of death for which he intimated his desire.

Upon hearing the perfectly natural answer of the judges, that the meaning of the words of Jesus was diametrically opposed to the accusation, and that there was nothing in them to warrant his condemnation, Pilate employed his final resource for prejudicing the trial, *viz.*, the deposition of a purchased traitorous informer. This miserable wretch —who was, no doubt, Judas—accused Jesus formally, of having incited the people to rebellion.

Then followed a scene of unsurpassed sublimity. When Judas gave his testimony, Jesus, turning toward him, and giving him his blessing, says: "Thou wilt find mercy, for what thou hast said did not come out from thine own heart!" Then, addressing himself to the governor: "Why dost thou lower thy dignity, and teach thy inferiors to tell falsehood, when without doing so it is in thy power to condemn an innocent man?"

Words touching as sublime! Jesus Christ here manifests all the grandeur of his soul by pardoning his betrayer, and he reproaches Pilate with having resorted to such means, unworthy of his dignity, to attain his end.

This keen reproach enraged the governor,

and caused him to completely forget his position, and the prudent policy with which he had meant to evade personal responsibility for the crime he contemplated. He now imperiously demanded the conviction of Jesus, and, as though he intended to make a display of his power, to overawe the judges, ordered the acquittal of the two thieves

The judges, seeing the injustice of Pilate's demand, that they should acquit the malefactors and condemn the innocent Jesus, refused to commit this double crime against their consciences and their laws. But as they could not cope with one who possessed the authority of final judgment, and saw that he was firmly decided to rid himself, by whatever means, of a man who had fallen under the suspicions of the Roman authorities, they left him to himself pronounce the verdict for which he was so anxious. In order, however, that the people might not suspect them of sharing the responsibility for such unjust judgment, which would not readily have been forgiven, they, in leaving the court, performed the ceremony of washing their hands, symbolizing the affirmation that they were clean of the blood of the innocent Jesus, the beloved of the people.

About ten years ago, I read in a German journal, the *Fremdenblatt*, an article on Judas, wherein the author endeavored to demonstrate that the informer had been the best friend of Jesus. According to him, it was out of love for his master that Judas betrayed him, for he put blind faith in the words of the Saviour, who said that his kingdom would arrive after his execution. But after seeing him on the cross, and having waited in vain for the resurrection of Jesus, which he expected to immediately take place, Judas, not able to bear the pain by which his heart was torn, committed suicide by hanging himself. It would be profitless to dwell upon this ingenious product of a fertile imagination.

To take up again the accounts of the Gospels and the Buddhistic chronicle, it is very possible that the bribed informer was really Judas, although the Buddhistic version is silent on this point. As to the pangs of conscience which are said to have impelled the informer to suicide, I must say that I give no credence to them. A man capable of committing so vile and cowardly an action as that of making an infamously false accusation against his friend, and this, not out of a spirit of jealousy, or for revenge, but to gain a handful of shekels! such a man is, from the psychic point of view, of very little worth. He ignores honesty and conscience, and pangs of remorse are unknown to him.

It is presumable that the governor treated him as is sometimes done in our days, when it is deemed desirable to effectually conceal state secrets known to men of his kind and presumably unsafe in their keeping. Judas probably was simply hanged, by Pilate's order, to prevent the possibility of his some day revealing that the plot of which Jesus was a victim had been inspired by the authorities.

On the day of the execution, a numerous detachment of Roman soldiers was placed around the cross to guard against any attempt by the populace for the delivery of him who was the object of their veneration

In this occurrence Pilate gave proof of his extraordinary firmness and resolution.

But though, owing to the precautions taken by the governor, the anticipated revolt did not occur, he could not prevent the people, after the execution, mourning the ruin of their hopes, which were destroyed, together with the last scion of the race of David. All the people went to worship at Jesus' grave. Although we have no precise information concerning the occurrences of the first few days following the Passion, we could, by some probable conjectures, re-construct the scenes which must have taken place.

It stands to reason that the Roman Cæsar's clever lieutenant, when he saw that Christ's grave became the centre of universal lamentations and the subject of national grief, and feared that the memory of the righteous victim might excite the discontent of the people and raise the whole country against the foreigners' rule, should have employed any effective means for the removal of this rallying-point, the mortal remains of Jesus. Pilate began by having the body buried. For three days the soldiers who were stationed on guard at the grave, were exposed to all kinds of insults and injuries on the part of the people who, defying the danger, came in multitudes to mourn the great martyr. Then Pilate ordered his soldiers to remove the body at night, and to bury it clandestinely in some other place, leaving the first grave open and the guard withdrawn from it, so that the people could see that Jesus had disappeared. But Pilate missed his end; for when, on the following morning, the Hebrews did not find the corpse of their master in the sepulchre, the superstitious and miracle-accepting among them thought that he had been resurrected.

How did this legend take root? We cannot say. Possibly it existed for a long time in a latent state and, at the beginning, spread only among the common people; perhaps the ecclesiastic authorities of the Hebrews looked with indulgence upon this innocent belief, which gave to the oppressed a shadow of revenge on their oppressors. However it be, the day when the legend of the resurrection finally became known to all, there was no one to be found strong enough to demonstrate the impossibility of such an occurrence.

Concerning this resurrection, it must be remarked that, according to the Buddhists, the soul of the just Issa was united with the eternal Being, while the Evangelists insist upon the ascension of the body. It seems to me, however, that the Evangelists and the Apostles have done very well to give the description of the resurrection which they have agreed upon, for if they had not done so, *i. e.*, if the miracle had been given a less material character, their preaching would not have had, in the eyes of the nations to whom it was presented, that divine authority, that avowedly supernatural character, which has clothed Christianity, until our time, as the only religion capable of elevating the human race to a state of sublime enthusiasm, suppressing its savage instincts, and bringing it nearer to the grand and simple nature which God has bestowed, they say, upon that feeble dwarf called man.

EXPLANATORY NOTES.

Chapter III.

§§ 3, 4, 5, 7.

The histories of all peoples show that when a nation has reached the apogee of its military glory and its wealth, it begins at once to sink more or less rapidly on the declivity of moral degeneration and decay. The Israelites having, among the first, experienced this law of the evolution of nations, the neighboring peoples profited by the decadence of the then effeminate and debauched descendants of Jacob, to despoil them.

§ 8.

The country of Romeles, *i. e.*, the fatherland of Romulus; in our days, Rome.

§§ 11, 12.

It must be admitted that the Israelites, in spite of their incontestable wit and intelligence, seem to have only had regard for the present. Like all other Oriental peoples, they only in their misfortunes remembered the faults of their past, which they each time had to expiate by centuries of slavery.

Chapter IV.

§ 6.

As it is easy to divine, this verse refers to Joseph, who was a lineal descendant from King David. Side by side with this somewhat vague indication may be placed the following passages from the Gospels :

—" The angel of the Lord appeared unto him in a dream, saying, Joseph, thou son of David, fear not to take unto thee Mary thy wife" . . . (Matt. i, 20.)

—" And the multitudes that went before, and that followed, cried, saying, Hosanna to the son of David" (Matt. xxi, 9).

—" To a virgin espoused to a man whose name was Joseph, of the house of David ;" . . (Luke i, 27.)

—" And the Lord God shall give unto him the throne of his father David ;" . . . (Luke i, 32.)

—" And Jesus himself began to be about thirty years of age, being (as was supposed) the son of Joseph, which was the son of Heli, . . . which was the son of Nathan, which was the son of David" (Luke iii, 23–31).

§ 7.

Both the Old and the New Testaments teach that God promised David the rehabilitation of his throne and the elevation to it of one of his descendants.

§§ 8, 9.

—"And the child grew, and waxed strong in spirit, filled with wisdom: and the grace of God was upon him."

—"And it came to pass, that after three days they found him in the temple, sitting in the midst of the doctors, both hearing them, and asking them questions."

—"And all that heard him were astonished at his understanding and answers."

—"And he said unto them, How is it that ye sought me? wist ye not that I must be about my Father's business?"

—"And Jesus increased in wisdom and stature, and in favor with God and man" (Luke ii, 40, 46, 47, 49, 52).

Chapter V

§ 1.

"Sind," a Sanscrit word, which has been modified by the Persians into Ind. "Arya," the name given in antiquity to the inhabitants of India; signified first "man who cultivates the ground" or "cultivator." Anciently it had a purely ethnographical signification; this appellation assumed later on a religious sense, notably that of "man who believes."

§ 2.

Luke says (i, 80): "And the child grew, and waxed strong in spirit, and was in the deserts till the day of his shewing unto Israel." The Evangelists say that Jesus was in the desert, the Buddhists explain this version of the Gospels by indicating where Jesus was during his absence from Judea. According to them he crossed the Sind, a name which, properly spoken, signifies "the river" (Indus). In connection with this word it is not amiss to note that many Sanscrit words in passing into the Persian language underwent the same transformation by changing the "s" into "h;" per example:

Sapta (in Sanscrit), signifying seven—*hafta* (in Persian) ;

Sam (Sanscrit), signifying equal—*ham* (Persian) ;

Mas (Sanscrit), meaning mouth—*mah* (Persian) ; *Sur* (Sanscrit), meaning sun—*hur* (Persian) ; *Das* (Sanscrit), meaning ten—*Dah* (Persian) ; *Loco citato*—and those who believed in the god Djain.

There exists, even yet, on the peninsula of Hindustan, a cult under the name of Djainism, which forms, as it were, a link of union between Buddhism and Brahminism, and its devotees teach the destruction of all other beliefs, which they declare contaminated with falsehood. It dates as far back as the seventh century, B. C. Its name is derived from Djain (conqueror), which it assumed as the symbol of its triumph over its rivals.

§ 4.

Each of the eighteen Puranas is divided into five parts, which, besides the canonical laws, the rites and the commentaries upon the creation, destruction and resurrection of the universe. deal with theogony, medicine, and even the trades and professions.

Chapter VI.

§ 12.

Owing to the intervention of the British, the human sacrifices, which were principally offered to Kali, the goddess of death, have now entirely ceased. The goddess Kali is represented erect, with one foot upon the dead body of a man, whose head she holds in one of her innumerable hands, while with the other hand she brandishes a bloody dagger. Her eyes and mouth, which are wide open, express passion and cruelty.

Chapter VIII.

§§ 3, 4.

Zoroaster lived 550 years before Jesus. He founded the doctrine of the struggle between light and darkness, a doctrine which is fully expounded in the Zend-Avesta (Word of God), which is written in the Zend language, and, according to tradition, was given to him by an angel from Paradise.

According to Zoroaster we must worship Mithra (the sun), from whom descend Ormuzd, the god of good, and Ahriman, the god of evil. The world will end when Ormuzd has triumphed over his rival, Ahriman, who will then return to his original source, Mithra.

Chapter X.

§ 16.

According to the Evangelists, Jesus was born in Bethlehem, which the Buddhistic version confirms, for only from Bethlehem, situated at a distance of about seven kilometres from Jerusalem, could the walls of this latter city be seen.

Chapter XI.

§ 15.

The doctrine the Redemptor is, almost in its entirety, contained in the Gospels. As to the transformation of men into children, it is especially known from the conversation that took place between Jesus and Nicodemus.

Chapter XII.

§ 1.

—"Tell us therefore, What thinkest thou? Is it lawful to give tribute unto Cæsar, or not?" (Matt. xxii, 17.)

§ 3.

—"Then saith he unto them, Render therefore unto Cæsar the things which are Cæsar's; and unto God the things that are God's. (Matt. xxii, 21 ; *et. al.*)

Chapter XIV

§ 3.

According to the Buddhistic belief, the terrestrial buddhas after death, lose consciousness of their independent existence and unite with the eternal Spirit.

§§ 10, 11.

Here, no doubt, reference is made to the activity of the Apostles among the neighboring peoples ; an activity which could not have passed unnoticed at that epoch, because of the great results which followed the preaching of the new religious doctrine of love among nations whose religions were based upon the cruelty of their gods.

. . . . . .

Without permitting myself indulgence in great dissertations, or too minute analysis upon each verse, I have thought it useful to accompany my work with these few little explanatory notes, leaving it to the reader to take like trouble with the rest.

FINIS.